The Golden-Bristled Boar

The Golden-Bristled BOAR

LAST FEROCIOUS BEAST

OF THE FOREST

JEFFREY GREENE

UNIVERSITY OF VIRGINIA PRESS | CHARLOTTESVILLE

University of Virginia Press
© 2011 by Jeffrey Greene
All rights reserved
Printed in the United States of America on acid-free paper

First published 2011

1 3 5 7 9 8 6 4 2

Library of Congress Cataloging-in-Publication Data
Greene, Jeffrey, 1952–
The golden-bristled boar : last ferocious beast
of the forest / Jeffrey Greene.
p. cm.
Includes bibliographical references and index.
ISBN 978-0-8139-3103-6 (cloth : alk. paper)
ISBN 978-0-8139-3128-9 (e-book)
1. Wild boar hunting — History.   2. Wild boar hunting —
Southern States — History.   3. Wild boar — Mythology.
4. Wild boar in art.   I. Title.
SK305.W5G74 2011   599.63'32 — dc22
2010034082

For Mary
and
Charles Siebert

Brokk then brought out his treasures. . . . To Frey he gave the boar, remarking that night or day it could race across the sky and over the sea better than any other mount. Furthermore, night would never be so murky nor the worlds of darkness so shadowy that the boar would not provide light wherever it went, so bright was the shining of its bristles.

— Snorri Sturluson, *The Prose Edda,*

trans. Byock

Contents

The Golden-Bristled Boar

Chapter One

La Compagnie

I F YOU ARE lucky enough, maybe even once or twice in a dozen years, your route, a solitary communal road in Burgundy, for example, will suddenly transect the path of a different tribe, a strict society in motion, one that shares the same terrain as you but one that awakens at dusk and flourishes in implausible obscurity, given its size, numbers, and vast distribution. It's hard to prepare for the moment when a train of up to twenty vigorous wild boars of varying ages and bulk moves rapidly as a unit out of the variegated light in chestnut, oak, and *charme* trees and then crosses toward the opening of a plowed field or one left fallow or one with corn. They bolt across a drainage ditch, each silhouette with tall, muscular shoulders, a short, powerful neck, enormous head, and almost trunklike snout.

The society is matriarchal; the largest and oldest female always leads. Three or four sizable females follow her manifold signals: the tail straight with alarm, ears alert, teeth clacking. Between them are one- or two-year-olds rushing into a gallop. The younger ones are called *rousses* in French for their reddish color. The smallest, with watermelonlike stripes, are called *marcassins*. Older males are systematically banished to roam singularly until winter and mating with a distant group, assuring genetic diversity. This society is called a sounder in English or *la compagnie* in French.

The road could be almost any among the mixed farms and small forests, the fecund *paysage* of which the French are rightly proud, but the one I'm describing is the rue des Postillons, hardly wider than the old

La compagnie (a sounder) of wild boar. (© Alexis Courraud)

postal carriages that once traveled to villages of eighty to a hundred inhabitants at most — Breteau, Champoulet, and Dammarie-en-Puisaye.
It forks off from the middle of our village, following the south bank
of the Loing River. The fields are lined with neglected apple and pear
trees and the modest homes of tenant farmers. Chateau owners still
manage many of the forests. Along this road, I began my encounters
with wild boars but then chose the surroundings of a nearby pond in
the woods, where I'd observe them into the early hours of the morning. I say "encounters" because they are not animals one can commune
with in the wild or even observe easily. After all, boars have come to
epitomize modifiers that mix mystery and myth — nocturnal, elusive,
and beastly. They appear in thrilling moments, "beautiful monsters,"
as the poet Robinson Jeffers called them. Gamey and bristled, tusking
the earth in darkness, no other animal seems a greater emissary of the
wild on a continent long devoid of wilderness.

And yet boars fattened on autumn bounty of acorns and chestnuts
have signified prosperity and resurrection in the darkest time of the

year. The sacrifice and the splitting of the boar followed by a feast became the luminous center of winter festivities in northern Europe, and the animal took a place in religious cosmology. Of the great mythic boars, my favorite is Gullinbursti, a precursor of Santa's reindeer. Forged by dwarfs, the golden-bristled boar was a gift to the fertility god Frey. The boar served as Frey's soaring mount, its bristles lighting up the murky ends of the universe. The forest's black beasts came to symbolize the returning light of the new year.

Chapter Two

The Gift

O N A TYPICAL fogbound evening, a Sunday just days before Christmas, our neighbor Monsieur Delanoe, a lean, elegant-looking Frenchman with striking white hair and neatly trimmed beard, presented me — I should say dropped in my lap — an unexpected gift: a black plastic garbage sack wrapped around an enormous piece of meat. It turned out to be the weighty shoulder, ribs, and loin of a *sanglier,* as wild boars are called here. My wife, Mary, and I didn't know it yet, but the near-black bristled fur was still attached, contrasting with the deep red flesh. We would discover a dreadful wound in the lower ribs below the shoulder. We were unaccustomed to receiving the carcass of a large animal, or even a large unbutchered fraction of one, as a gift. Undoubtedly we looked bewildered at an offering that resembled a body bag, an impression reinforced by the fact that boars in our part of Burgundy are human size, although there are even larger exceptions.

We had come to the Delanoes' bearing our own gift, namely a case of wine. The Delanoes lived in a low-income house at the end of our small pasture, their yard populated with inert farm machinery and cannibalized vans half-visible in the darkening haze. Delanoe, a consummate woodsman, was a chivalric throwback: handsome, gentlemanly, and perpetually clad in hunting clothes. Madame Delanoe, hefty with black, unkempt hair, was animated and personable, possessed with the near supernatural strength of French country folks. I knew because I'd unloaded and stacked two cords of firewood alongside of her, and unlike me she appeared hardly taxed afterward, talking freely while casually rolling a cigarette. Monsieur Delanoe systematically cut the spring and autumn hay in our pasture and maintained our few trees without ever presenting us with a bill. I would thank him, and he would answer with a dismissive, "C'est normal." The code he lived by demanded that he help neighbors in need, no hesitation, no questions asked, no interest in reciprocity. Mary and I lived and worked in Paris, enjoying the country on all-too-short weekends. We relied on our neighbors to keep an eye on our place, even though my mother had moved in full-time. The only recompense we could offer Monsieur Delanoe, if you could call it recompense, was to leave our apple trees at his disposal, which meant, don't let the good fruit go to waste if you can use it. This sort of arrangement was intuitively suitable. The Delanoes each autumn collected the apples and made what they called fermented cider, better known as water of life, a crystal-clear drink locally distilled with phantom aromas of apples or pears.

We respected Monsieur Delanoe's code but still felt, after the years passed without his coming with a bill, that we should pay him something for all his services, and so under the guise of dropping off our tokens of the Joyeuses Fêtes, we arrived at the Delanoes' home only to receive a major fraction of an animal carcass. We passed the rigorous inspection of a fox terrier and a Breton spaniel, and then were welcomed by the Delanoes themselves; the television was stuck on a French game show; an enormous fish tank glowed with an ultraviolet tint; and heads of deer, fox, and wild boar were displayed on the walls. An apéritif liqueur, *du jaune,* was generously poured, wafting with anise and herbs. Between the animals on the wall, there were cases replete with an armory for bringing down creatures of all sizes, including a prominently displayed bolt-action German K98k Mauser, "1944" carved on its stock. Monsieur Delanoe explained with poignant understatement that the gun had been his father's prize. Our village in Burgundy had minor strategic interest to the Nazis since the Briare Canal passed through, linking the Seine and the Loire rivers.

We couldn't help inquiring about hunting in the region where the sport was outrageously popular and where Monsieur Delanoe managed and stocked wild ducks and pheasants on nearby property owned by a Parisian. The owner took just a small percentage of the *actions de chasse* (organized hunting). On a number of occasions, Delanoe, his white hair luminous, would wave to me from the misty, corn-stubbled fields with fully outfitted men and their busy zigzagging spaniels. Our curiosity led to an outpouring of information regarding the bureaucracy of local hunting.

"First, you have to purchase bracelets in advance for the wild boar you hope to shoot. That's fifty euros. Hunting licenses need to be validated each year, and they are anything but cheap, around four hundred euros a year if you want to hunt both large and small game. Then you pay to join a hunting association and often for *actions* on private property. Every large animal taken has to be tagged, or you could receive an enormous fine or even be sent to prison."

The penalties seemed severe, but I would hear later that for poaching frogs the fine can reach ten thousand euros and possibly getting your car confiscated.

Delanoe understood that Americans, with their vast tracts of land, didn't have the same restrictive heritage. For poaching in the royal forests of the Old Regime, you could lose your head. Among the lighter punishments were castration, blinding, and the removal of hands and feet. Many of the forests in France are still associated with chateaux and remain an important source of income through hunting and selective lumber-cutting leases.

I assured Monsieur Delanoe that American hunting had its rules and restrictions too, although at the time I hadn't the faintest idea what they were. Hunters were reputed to be unpredictable. Even their dogs have caused accidents, stepping on the trigger of a neglected firearm. France isn't immune to the madness of hunting incidents. A French hunter made news when his irate potshot downed a marine helicopter training over his favorite hunting copse. While this is an extreme example, the annual average of two hundred accidental shootings was enough to inspire the Office National de la Chasse et de la Faune Sauvage to institute compulsory education programs in hunting safety. A prospective hunter is required to take a twenty-one-question test and score at least sixteen questions right. Out of curiosity, I took a practice test — in French, of course — and, no great test taker, I surprised myself by scoring nineteen. I had never hunted or for that matter fired a gun in my life.

The conversation moved on to the overpopulation of wild boars. During hunting season, boars will on occasion run into homes and schools and demolish the furniture and classroom computers. Veterinarians find themselves sewing up the same dogs each weekend, and a boar had even bitten Monsieur Delanoe, leaving an odd scar above his hip. He considered it a mark of folly rather than valor, having presumed a boar was dead only to find that it wasn't. Delanoe learned his lesson, or relearned it, and demonstrated to me his customary defensive move, turning his side to an imagined boar, which instinctively slashes or gouges upward with its tusks. Turning your hip supposedly protects the vulnerable inner thigh and the femoral artery. When attacked by other animals, a male boar can readily pierce an adversary's pulmonary cavity or abdomen, the most common lethal injuries for hunting dogs. The females may not have tusks nearly as large as a male's, but they can bite or simply bowl you over. And they can be more volatile if they perceive a threat to their piglets. Tackling a full-grown boar is a formidable task for even the largest predators, an academic point given that the boar's natural predators have all but vanished from Europe and, for that matter, from the five other continents they inhabit.

Delanoe left the table and fetched the whole side of a sanglier wrapped in black plastic. He deposited this weighty gift into my arms while Madame Delanoe instructed Mary: "You must marinate it in red wine for at least a day, sometimes two days. Put in red wine, onions, carrots, peppercorns, and *laurier.*" She went back to the refrigerator and packed another plastic bag with two pheasants, a male with a luminous green head and pure red about the eyes and a female, the gradient browns of fallen leaves and winter grasses.

We were accustomed to receiving gifts. Vegetables, flowers, partridges, and bottles of wine would simply appear on our windowsill. This kind of generosity between neighbors was simply a part of country life, and more often than not it was poorer neighbors who gave most freely. We as foreigners were a source of curiosity, particularly because we had purchased a deserted eighteenth-century presbytery that is one of the village's principal historic buildings. What seemed to us the epitome of charm, a stone house with large windows and a moss-covered roof, to the locals was a veritable nightmare of leaks, rotted beams, bats, spiders, and a long succession of religious ghosts. A former church graveyard even extended into our backyard. The local people wanted nothing to do with it. Mary and I had been carrying on an improbable transatlantic affair, and it was characteristic of our impulsive natures to buy a presbytery we couldn't afford and end up hosting a country picnic wedding for ourselves on its grounds. My mother, falling in love with the building at the wedding, took early retirement and managed to become the first full-time resident in the old priest's house in fifteen years, all to our great surprise.

Although the locals lavished gifts on us and praised us for having the courage to restore the forsaken house, we had never before received a wild boar carcass. I began romanticizing our gift as an act of primal generosity, almost tribal, a ritual sharing of the fruit of the hunt: wild boar meat. For our ancestors, tribal sharing was at the essence of survival, whereas the Delanoes in the twenty-first century probably had more boar meat than they knew what to do with and reasoned that for the only Americans living in the area, butchering a wild boar would be an unparalleled adventure.

Little did the Delanoes suspect nor I that their gift would initiate a journey of revelations for me. After our evening together, I began asking neighbors about wild boars, which in turn led me to professors of forestry, directors of hunting preserves, butchers, cooks, veterinarians, artists, and hunters. Almost everyone wanted to share tales about boars. My curiosity extended to other countries, then continents. The extraordinary relationship between man and the wild boar through the ages, the boar's role in civilization and culture, began with the primacy

Wild boar leaping into water. (© Stéphan Levoye)

of the hunt and the myths and rituals associated with it. Art, cuisine, and aristocratic privilege naturally followed. To begin understanding this relationship, I needed only to look in my own backyard. It turned out we were living in one of the most densely populated boar areas in Europe.

From the last week of September until the last day of February, a war is waged on the wild animals in our region, which is otherwise so peaceful that in winter it is regarded politely by our more sophisticated friends as the dark end of the world. Each Sunday for five full months, the gunfire, horns, and shouts echo so close to the Loing River and the Briare Canal that it seems as if the hunt is taking place in the very streets of Rogny-les-Sept-Ecluses, our village of 750 inhabitants, five bars, and one pharmacy. In the scant December light and with the valley erased by fog, I get the impression that shots are fired in our small orchard next to an eleventh-century church, where we've seen pheasants, deer, and wildcats blundering into the village unawares.

Family farms still populate our landscape, the fields nurturing a rotation of rape, mustard, corn, wheat, and sunflowers; or pasturing cows, ponies, goats, and sheep. The land is broken up by copses and extensive wooded areas that obscure a surprising number of small ponds and marshes and in autumn harbor a wealth of mushrooms, chestnuts, hazelnuts, and acorns, all among the preferred fare of wild boars. But what has astounded me since buying a house in France is the population density of wild animals here, one that made the New England woods where I grew up seem all but vacant. I've never taken a drive or walk on which I didn't encounter beautiful animals of all sorts, often *gibier,* or game. Of course, many of the pheasants, partridges, and ducks are released by farmers compelled to satisfy hunters who pay for *actions.* Of the released animals, the pheasants and partridges appear bewildered, almost paralyzed by the vastness of the great outdoors after being raised in wire pens. The survivors adapt. Like fox, martens, wildcats, and hawks, the wild boars benefit from the released animals, raiding nests, devouring eggs and hatchlings.

While hunting as a sport has never appealed to me, I recognize the bonds, rituals, and instincts that hunting proffers, usually among men, although women in France have their own hunting organization: l'Association Nationale de la Chasse au Féminin. The sport is inextricably bound to European and Asian aristocratic tradition, pageantry, and glory, while in America the hunter, in the tradition of James Fenimore Cooper's *Deerslayer,* is glorified as a self-reliant agent of the natural world, possessing near mystical powers of common sense and honesty. That said, tycoons originally imported the purer European boars to North Carolina and then California for hunting reserves, creating a sport of social privilege in its own right. Many of the hunters I've come to know have turned out to be ardent naturalists and environmentalists, tuned in spiritually and sensually to the landscape and behavior of their quarry. Certainly hunters have been among our best nature writers and artists as hunting mixes observation and passion. In the case of boars, considered a plague in France, hunting is a respected service to the farmers and winemakers, who tally enormous damages. However, boars and feral pigs inspire a range of hunting methods, particularly in the United States and Australia, where men tackle boars with no more than a knife, thus evoking the Special Forces or perhaps Jim Bowie. Hunters post photographs of themselves on the Internet, a bloody knife brandished triumphantly, the vanquished boar sprawled in a truck bed.

Most of my French friends don't quibble with their consciences when it comes to eating, and hunting is practiced nationwide, its modern application often devoid of any mystique. From the major highways to Paris, just outside of the suburbs, you can see the traditional line of hunters marching systematically through the corn stubble, dogs weaving ahead; or you see them deployed around a stand of trees while game is flushed from one side by a line of men called *rabatteurs,* or beaters. They provide a diversion for the rest of us stuck bumper to bumper in the Sunday reentry into the région parisienne, factories and high-tension wires looming.

Our country house is situated in ideal boar territory, the Puisaye, a region of low, rolling hills, forests, and chateaux of the Knights Templar in northeastern Burgundy between the Loire and the Yonne rivers. While the Puisaye is only ninety miles from Paris, it remains relatively undiscovered by foreign visitors. Even the French hardly know the region unless they've read Colette's memoirs of her early years or taken barge vacations on the Briare Canal, passing through or docking in our village center.

Conjecture has it that the word "Puisaye" is derived from combining the Celtic words *poy* and *saga* to signify "land of ponds and woods." Since boars, like the domestic pig, do not produce sweat and are keen on ridding themselves of ticks and lice, they revel in the streams and muddy ponds that are plentiful in our quiet wooded region. They leave telltale wallows called *souilles* along with other ubiquitous signs of their presence: boar runs, rubbings on trees, tracks, droppings, and, above all, whole stretches of roadside rooted up. Still, you will only see a sanglier in the wild when it is flushed out of a thicket, or glimpsed by the canal in the evening or the fields in the early-morning mist. The males, when not in rut, are solitary; thus the French name *sanglier* — singular — which I had always wrongly associated with *sang,* blood or bloody.

Despite the reputed epidemic of wild boars, it took me nearly twenty years actually to see one in nature. When I mentioned this to my friend Muriel, she looked at me with disbelief. Muriel, a vegetarian, ironically sells high-quality Alsatian *charcuterie,* including *saucisse de sanglier,* at six local village markets, requiring her to drive during early-morning hours almost daily. "My God, sangliers are the worst! They have small eyes that don't glow on the road like other animals. There's no warning. I've crashed two vans into them already." The number of automobile accidents attributed to wild boars has reached a stunning 14,500 per year in France. They cause more accidents than any other large game, even managing to damage trains. Insurance companies are obliged to offer special large animal–collision coverage.

As it turned out, my first encounter with boars was a near-accident on a commune road where the woods grew dense. I blundered into the full drama of a wild boar hunt, announced by a yellow caution sign with an image of a dashing wild boar and large red print: "Danger! Boar hunt in progress." The hunters use the road as a clearing for a clean shot. I never took these signs seriously until I narrowly avoided hitting two massive boars charging across the road while a hunter beside my car fired out of frustration rather than any hope of a kill. Being caught up in the commotion of wild pigs and gunfire resulted in another near miss. A black-and-white springer spaniel, known better for "springing" birds than torrid pursuit of boars, paid no heed to my oncoming car. In one chaotic moment that brought me to a full halt, I saved the lives of two wild boars and a dog, though dogs often become victims in a boar hunt. The wild pigs get the worst of it; they rarely live long enough to experience a natural death. To the chagrin of hunting purists in France looking for a satisfying trophy, 80 percent of the boars taken are juveniles, a year and a half old or less. Only 15 percent of the males reach two to three years of age, although in captivity they can live up to twenty-five years. A six- or seven-year-old boar in the wild ranks as a marvel of good luck or near supernatural cunning.

While derailing a hunt was not the ideal way to observe boars in nature, the action was exhilarating. Wild boars are dramatic, simultaneously homely and majestic, possessing explosive strength and speed. Older males can have formidable tusks, modified canine teeth actually. They are so striking in appearance that cultures exaggerate them in primitive masks, for example, or in images depicting India's Vishnu in his boar incarnation, Varaha, saving our drowning planet by firmly balancing it on his snout. The curved, stubby upper tusks are called "whetters," and the fearsome protruding lower tusks are known as "cutters." Given the configuration and the articulation of the jaws, whetters keep the cutters spear-tip sharp. Impressive enough in themselves, the tusks commonly serve as hunters' trophies mounted like so many crescent moons lined up on stained wood or a velvet-covered plaque.

Even though 99 percent of the time a wild boar will flee from you, it's impossible not to feel tension in your diaphragm on hearing deep grunts and thrashing in the underbrush. Boars are masterly at concealing themselves. Still, that 1 percent makes world news: breaking into apartments in Berlin, attacking a kindergarten in Kyoto, destroying farmhouses in France. Hungry boars wander into grocery stores, something that seems entirely understandable, given that they eat everything we do and much more. They shock customers with their surprise visits to liquor shops and department stores. They frequent discothèques where teenagers mollycoddle them with hamburgers and fries, and in Seoul boars come down from the mountains to drop by upscale hotels and palace grounds, causing outrage. Among their most annoying habits outside the forest is their prodigious digging for worms. The French have a word for it, *vermiller*, and in one night a compagnie is capable of laying waste to several golf course fairways and greens.

Until we brought home Delanoe's gift of half a boar, I hadn't given the animal serious thought. Having a rather small refrigerator, we had no choice but to butcher the meat to keep it fresh. Technically, being confronted with only a large fraction of a boar hardly counted as butchering; we had neither the formidable head to contend with nor the humanlike entrails to grow queasy over. Still, the unwrapped flesh took up our entire tiled kitchen counter.

With her background as a scientist and her methodical approach to

Chinese police remove a young wild boar from a train station. (© AFP)

life's challenges, Mary inspected the animal before offering a plan of action. She ran her fingertips along the bristles at the spine. "Let's keep the loin intact. This beautiful muscle here." She felt along the back where it tapered toward the hip, and tried unsuccessfully to pull back the tough skin from the red meat and partially visible backbone. She instinctively placed a finger on the wound through the lower ribs out of respect for the violence recorded there, a hole she could put her fist through.

Butchering the boar gave me an opportunity to study the structure of bones, muscles, tendons, and vessels. The dorsal vertebrae have exceptionally long and well-developed spinous processes, projecting bones that support a large muscle mass, providing extra power from the back and shoulders for plowing up the earth. The neck has only seven short vertebrae, again adding strength but limiting the boar's ability to move its head from side to side. Structure follows function. The meat itself throughout the body is deep-red muscle tissue containing extra myoglobin, a protein molecule designed to store additional oxygen. Clearly, the boar is built for pure power.

It's easy to understand artists cluttering their studios with skeletons, feathers, skins, shells, teeth, and claws, particularly when they are concerned with realism and precise renderings of anatomy. Some artists instinctively pursue the recommendation of Leon Battista Alberti in his fifteenth-century treatise *On Painting:* "It would be useful to isolate each bone of the animal, on this add its muscles, then clothe all of it with its flesh." The act of painting thus constitutes a reconstruction of the animal.

I visited a professional nature artist, Monsieur Olivier, whose house was completely hidden in a forest near our village. He was obsessed with all animals but above all wild boars, both hunting them and then rendering them in bronze castings as well as in paintings and drawings. His studio resembled an eccentric temple consecrated to pieces of animals. The cornices were morbidly lined with dozens of roe-deer skulls. An enormous mounted boar's head dominated the casting and printing room, and four boar skulls, boiled free of flesh, were lined up carefully on a table, their whetters and cutters on full display. One skull came from a pet boar he had raised illegally in his yard years ago. A cigar stub lodged between his fingers, Monsieur Olivier explained the structure of the long snout, a special nasal bone providing support during rooting. He opened the jaw to show the wear on the teeth, estimated the boar's age, and demonstrated the self-sharpening action of the tusks. I asked what fascinated him about boars. "Passion," he responded bluntly. "The animal stirs fear and passion."

Monsieur Olivier's bronze boars brought to mind one of the world's most adored works of animal art, Pietro Tacca's Italian High Renaissance sculpture known as *Porcellino.* The life-sized, meticulously rendered boar sculpture occupied for centuries a place of honor in Florence's Mercato Nuovo until crowds began to destroy it, patting its snout

Merchant stealing the fateful rose for his daughter Beauty, illustration
by Walter Crane from *Beauty and the Beast* (London and New York:
George Routledge and Sons, 1874). (Department of Special Collections,
Charles E. Young Research Library, UCLA)

for good luck. *Porcellino* offers a special paradox: adoring tourists photograph themselves with the boar, yet the animal is widely considered not
just unlovable but repulsive. After all, boars shovel their snouts through
mud and earth with the efficiency of a rototiller. They supplement their
largely vegetarian diets with everything children conjure up to revolt
each other: slugs, grubs, worms, and toads, the general rule being, "if it
has a calorie they'll eat it." The *New Yorker* writer Ian Frazier goes a step
further, describing them as "bristled vacuum-cleaner bags attached to

snouts." In the public imagination, they are immensely distant from the elegance of horses, the majesty of lions and tigers, and the shrewdness and wonder of bears, wolves, and foxes. Those of us who live near them on the six continents they inhabit know that they secrete themselves in earthen lairs during the daytime and at night commit a litany of crimes, among the less forgivable of which are ravaging food plots in desperately poor countries, eating eggs of endangered sea turtles, and rooting up rare plant species.

Perhaps because the wild boar is so alien to our affections and our ideas of beauty and grace, it is also regarded by many as the consummate beast, often referred to in France as the *bête noire*. The boar serves as a model for the beast in *Beauty and the Beast*. The aroused boar earns unquestionable respect in the hunt: readying to defend itself like no other animal, it is iconic. It is no surprise that the wild boar was the preferred adversary of Hercules, a formidable wound-giver to Ulysses, and the killer of Adonis, Aphrodite's lover.

Once we had butchered Monsieur Delanoe's boar into manageable pieces, I cleaned up the shoulder for a roast, and Mary worked meticulously on the ribs to prepare Ziploc bags full of meat scraps for stew or sauce. We were only guessing, dreaming really, about the sorts of meals we'd make besides a Christmas loin. The fact was that we knew nothing about preparing boar dishes or, for that matter, about boars themselves. I developed the urge to find them at night at a place where Monsieur Delanoe said he hunted them and Monsieur Olivier confirmed they were plentiful. I wanted to chronicle my encounters with the "beautiful monsters" that Robinson Jeffers described in his poem "Steelhead, Wild Pig, and the Fungus" as bristling "like a hedge at midnight, full of fecundity" and possessing "long naked / Knives in their jaws." I'm the last person to be interested in experiencing personal danger, but I wanted to get to know "the beast that arouses passions" in our gentle woods.

Chapter Three

Field Dressing

IRST YOU HAVE to make sure that the boar is dead," Jean-Pierre Bajon, our butcher, helpfully explained to us. I'd heard this warning before, and Monsieur Delanoe had an impressive moonlike scar on his hip to remind him of the danger. "Sometimes you have to shoot them again. Then, before anything else, if it's a male, particularly an older male, you cut off its testicles. You have to cut them off very, very quickly. If you don't, the flesh will taste of urine."

Having been initiated inadvertently into the world of butchering, Mary and I asked a genuine French expert about dressing sanglier. Because we had decided to make wild boar the center of our holiday dinner, we engaged Jean-Pierre, who happens to be one of the top ten butchers in Paris and a Club de la Nef d'Or laureate supported by the Chambre de Commerce et d'Industrie de Paris for his top-quality business. His boutique is on rue de l'Abbé Gregoire, a short street with a curious mixture of modest shops selling religious books, plumbing supplies, Asian furniture, and wedding dresses. Most notably, however, the street is the home of the Ecole Supérieure de Cuisine Française-Ferrandi, claiming to provide the best culinary training in France and therefore Europe. During holidays, especially at Christmas and New Year's, Jean-Pierre's shop is vibrant with orders and lively customers. The rotisserie set out on the sidewalk becomes a miniature Ferris wheel of chickens, ducks, and pieces of pork over glowing roasting elements, while his boutique window displays prepared foods: terrines, foie gras, sausages, sauerkraut, and *boudin blanc truffé*. Veal, pork, beef, and lamb, along with game during hunting season, are neatly arranged in a meat case. His top shelf features a variety of fowl you would be hard put to find elsewhere, including three or four breeds of chickens, capons, ducks, quail, pheasants, pigeons and, in season, even grouse. Many of the birds still sport some decorative plumage. If you peek into his refrigerated locker, you will see the hanging split carcasses of calves, cows, and lambs all being meticulously aged. Some mornings when I walk the dogs, I will stop to watch a white-hooded deliveryman hefting nearly half a cow on his back.

It might be my imagination, but it seems that most Parisians champion their butchers as the best in the city, if not the universe. We are no different. Ours was also generous enough to invite us into his home behind his boutique to discuss butchering a wild boar. This was not among his most common queries. We started with field dressing, an expression that for me evokes images of Oberon and Titania spreading glistening webs in a field rather than evisceration.

Jean-Pierre's home is modest, functional, and dark, his office situated just behind a frosted window that permits some light to filter through his boutique from the storefront. A stew simmered in his windowless kitchen next to the office. He was nursing a severe cold, cooking, serving customers, fielding phone calls, and taking time out to talk with us. A divorced father of three boys, he lives alone except for a black dog of indeterminable breed. What better life could be had than that of a butcher's dog? We sat at a round dining table in a room decorated by crockery, a pair of sculpted ducks, and various knickknacks, including a small D-Day plaque commemorating the American landing at Omaha Beach and a photograph of New York City. The dog leaned forcefully against my knee.

Jean-Pierre projects an odd mixture of warmth, flamboyance when fawning theatrically over his clients and a perfectionism bordering on brutality when he is scolding assistants or choosing his products. He is a smallish, athletic man with dark hair and blue eyes rather closely set together, increasing the look of intensity he wears when discussing his trade or advising a customer on the preparation of a cut of meat. He is a devotee of Harley Davidsons, coincidentally called "hogs" in the States. I'd see him on occasion fully garbed in black helmet and silver-studded black leather, wearing his trademark red bandana, a striking sight in Paris's Sixth Arrondissement. We learned that he has posed as a butcher in films starring Gérard Depardieu and the gorgeous Sophie Marceau. On the more professional side, he occasionally served as a cookbook consultant to the publisher Larousse.

Jean-Pierre had endeared himself to Mary before I lived with her. She'd spent a good part of one December in the hospital with a severely herniated disc and was released, still in pain, just a few days before Christmas. Mary's traditional Christmas dinner guests, oblivious to her physical ailments, called asking what she was planning to prepare for them. Not wanting to disappoint anyone or spend Christmas alone in misery, Mary, in turn, contacted Monsieur Bajon, who roasted two exceptional ducks for everyone, and Mary has sworn by him ever since.

Now, as Jean-Pierre described the steps of field dressing, we had wondered how male boar meat differed from that of a *laie,* the female boar. Hunters would tell us that even removing the testicles isn't enough to save the flavor of the meat if the animal is in rut, which isn't improbable given that rut peaks in December, coinciding with hunting season. Paradoxically, boar dishes rank high in the annual World Testicle Cooking Championships held in Serbia. While many are revolted at the mere suggestion, a macho cult of "extreme cuisine" has emerged, heavily promoted by offbeat chefs and cookbook authors such as Fergus Henderson, Heston Blumenthal, and Jerry Hopkins. In addition, there's moral satisfaction in thinking that consuming all parts of a beast honors the animal's noble, if unwilling, sacrifice. Boar testicles, considered a delicacy by some, are politely referred to in France as *les suites.*

And indeed, many things that might be considered extreme cuisine in America or Canada are prized in France, England, and Italy. If you spend much time in France, you are bound to come upon a specialty butcher shop called a *triperie* boasting an impressive display of brains, ears, tongues, cheeks, throats, thymus (sweetbreads), hearts, stomach (tripe), feet, and tails of pork, beef, and lamb. According to Jean-Pierre, the boar's head remains highly valued for cuisine. The head is cut off close to the shoulders to preserve neck meat, and the tongue is removed for use in a different dish. Once the ears are taken off, the head is blanched to ease the chore of scraping away the fur and then either put in a wine marinade for three days or stewed right away. The meat in the muzzle and cheeks was so esteemed through the ages that the presentation of a boar's head with an apple in its mouth or lemons skewered on its tusks, served on a silver or gold platter to a flourish of trumpets, became one of the oldest rituals associated with Christmas. Its origins may be Norse, the boar's head served with invocations to the god Frey to bestow riches in the new year, or Roman. But in England, Boar's Head Christmas is still remembered in a carol first published by Wynkyn de Worde in 1521:

> The bore's head in hande bring I,
> With garlandes gay and rosemary,
> I pray you all synge merely,
> *Qui estis in convivio.*

At Queen's College Oxford, celebration of Boar's Head Christmas is based as much on a slapstick tale as on ancient tradition. An Oxford student was purported to have saved himself from a charging wild boar by stuffing a volume of Aristotle down its throat and exclaiming "It is Greek; it cannot be read." (Aristotle, among many things an astute observer of nature, described in *History of Animals* the behavior of wild boars as "quick tempered, ferocious and unteachable.")

But back to our lesson in butchery arts. Jean-Pierre continued: "If you have the tools at hand and a means to hang the animal up by its back legs, then you can eviscerate a sanglier immediately. All good hunters do this. Then they take off the skin and put the carcass in a refrigerator right away. Sanglier spoils quickly because it is lean."

I'd seen a number of game-processing enterprises in Texas, and I asked Jean-Pierre if they existed in France. "Rarely," he replied. "Some slaughterhouses near the large forests with game parks can be called

Boar's Head Banquet: Chef of the Savoy Hotel, London.
(© E. Bacon/Getty Images)

in to render their services after a large kill — twenty, twenty-five, or thirty sangliers. They will come, pick up the animals, and process them immediately, and they have sufficient space in their cold rooms. Otherwise, no, not at all." Later, I would see the processed boars hanging in a cold room at one of the large hunting domains in Burgundy, a half-dozen boars, the fur still attached, hanging disturbingly by the chin from hooks.

It's important to eviscerate the animal quickly because the grains and other foods in the stomach and intestines begin to ferment almost immediately, threatening to foul the meat. The process is known as the *gralloch,* derived from Scottish Gaelic meaning "entrails." After flaying, hunters cut out and conserve edible innards — heart, liver, and kidneys. Later the head, skin, fur, and bristles will be removed, and the animal is often halved through the vertebrae and then quartered. The carcass is put in a refrigerated locker and can be kept for up to two weeks. More often though, hunters freeze the meat, which kills microbes and parasites.

We asked Jean-Pierre about the wisdom of aging boar meat. "If the sanglier is an older animal, it is better to age it some for tenderness and to reduce any bitterness," he replied. "But it is very delicate because meat that doesn't contain fat does not conserve well. After you skin and eviscerate game, you can't keep it for longer than twelve days. On the other hand, if you have meat that naturally contains fat, you can keep it twenty or thirty days, no problem. Of course, it has to be in a cold locker with good ventilation. Above all, it should have no humidity."

One of the most important practices butchers in Europe learn is that of aging meat, known in French as *faire rassir*. Similarly, the best cheese shops *affinent*, or carefully mature, cheese before presenting it for sale. Jean-Pierre compared the process to ripening fruit: "It's like a pear or a piece of fruit that's too green. We have to leave it to ripen for three to five days. Meat is exactly the same. It's necessary to look at it and smell it, later to touch it. We watch over the meat like a piece of fruit over time to be sure that it will be flavorful and tender."

"For an *escalope de veau*," he continued, "you need a higher heat, but veal that is too fresh can just give up its fluids, leaving the meat leathery. Boar is a little different. You can make wonderful escalope with boar, but you have to cook it at a lower heat to keep it moist."

The practice of aging meat, known also as conditioning, is ancient, probably not always out of choice, and allows natural enzymes to break down tougher connective tissue and muscle. It's common to age pheasants until the neck breaks naturally under the hung weight of the body. I can attest to the fact that this process hugely improves both flavor and tenderness, although it may seem unwise to most cautious modern diners, who fear salmonella poisoning. One of the most extreme forms of aging I've heard of is burying shark and ray in the earth to rot for up to six months, resulting in the pungent Icelandic delicacies *hakari* and *kaest skata* respectively. Both reputedly are more edible when followed by a throat scorcher called *Brennivin* — literally, "burning wine."

I had seen advertisements for boar ham, bacon, and terrines, and

I know that you can acquire boar meat on Amazon.com. Jean-Pierre explained that many of the cuts of boar are the same as pork. You save the liver, the knuckles, the feet, and the blood. So what is the difference between pork and boar?

"The sanglier is a wild pig, but it is not at all the same flesh as a domestic pig," Jean-Pierre explained. "It doesn't have the same consistency. The flesh on a pig is much lighter, less red. The sanglier has deep red flesh, and the flavor is much more pronounced, stronger. You have to cook sanglier differently, and you can't make the same variety of hams, rillettes, or sausages made from the intestines like andouille, which is very popular. It is like two different sorts of meat." Since rillettes is a terrine made with a large percentage of pork fat, it stands to reason that it would be difficult to make it with boar, but I wondered if the extreme-cuisine chefs would agree about the boar andouille. After all, the boar stomach and intestines don't look any different from those of a pig. Both have an unnerving resemblance to a human's single-stomach digestive system.

"Still, you butcher pork and sanglier practically in the same fashion," Jean-Pierre continued. "One butchers a sanglier to make a variety of roasts, ribs and chops, *escalopes,* sauces, and stews. If you come across an old *sanglier* that had been running around after the females, it's more difficult to prepare. Still you can make pâté, *civet* [a stew that often includes blood made from furred animals], and sausages, which are in great demand for their richer flavor. If you find a younger, tender boar, you can make exceptional dishes. You must look at and feel the meat to know how it can be used."

When we asked Jean-Pierre about how to cook the sanglier that we had butchered ourselves and planned to use for a holiday feast, he insisted that we bring it to his boutique. He refused to give any advice without examining the meat himself. We felt a bit odd carrying pieces of wild boar through Paris to have Jean-Pierre evaluate our amateur cuts. After pressing his fingers into the flesh, turning it over, trimming it, and squeezing it in his hands, Jean-Pierre pronounced our boar to be of top quality. "This is ideal for your fête," he assured us. We felt a little proud of our newfound prowess as butchers and grateful that Monsieur Delanoe had bestowed a true gift and not a castoff.

Discussing the sanglier led us further into Jean-Pierre's personal story. He had grown up on his parents' farm in the Sarthe, a region just to the east of Brittany known to outsiders for its major city, Le Mans. He never had a chance to complete his education, something he deeply regretted. He went to school when he was eight; his parents took him out to work on the farm at thirteen and a half. It was assumed he'd ultimately become an *agriculteur.* However, the prospect of farming for a lifetime didn't please Jean-Pierre, who didn't want to work seven days a week with no holidays, no rest, and no freedom. By fourteen, he dreamed of leaving the farm and finding his own vocation. At fifteen, he started a two-year apprenticeship in a butcher's shop in La Ferté-Bernard, where he practiced deboning and preparing meat, and by eighteen began choosing merchandise.

Being around farm animals throughout his childhood, Jean-Pierre had learned the traits of superior animals and his ability to recognize them became intuitive. "There are some who are more or less adept at choosing merchandise," he observed. "Some just don't have a notion. I mastered it. On occasion, I have found merchandise that shouldn't be sold or eaten. The veterinarians had missed it, so I'd call them in to show them. Most of the game that I buy for commerce comes from Rungis where a veterinarian's certificate is required. The government runs a control to make sure that you are selling the meat with the proper stamps. You have to pay attention to the healthiness of the meat you are selling because a client who gets sick might suspect it was from the hare, the pheasant, the partridge, or the boar you sold him. Above all with swine and avian flu around right now, you have to be attentive."

Wild boars carry a number of diseases and parasites that can infect humans: rabies, trichinosis, streptococcus, leptospirosis, brucellosis, liver flukes, and flu. Jean-Pierre warned that one should wear gloves when butchering a boar, leading Mary and me to exchange glances.

Rungis is the major food-distribution hub outside of Orly Airport that supplies fishmongers, butchers, vegetable and fruit grocers, and dairy merchants for Paris and outlying areas for hundreds of miles around. These products are distributed on a timetable beginning with fish at midnight and the other products in rotation through the early-morning hours. Jean-Pierre chooses his products at Rungis strictly on the criterion of quality. "Everyone at Rungis says that their products are the most beautiful. But I've been disappointed too many times."

Whenever we buy meat from Jean-Pierre, we ask for cooking instructions. It's easy to ruin a piece of meat, and Jean-Pierre's suggested cooking times and temperature are always on the mark. "It's not that I've been formally trained in cooking. I've learned by trying it myself, by careful reflection. I've learned the basis of various preparations and cooking times for the cuts of meat. It's easy for me to know how to cook a marcassin, for example. It just comes to me."

There are numerous traditional dishes that use what is called marcassin, young boar less than six months old. They are prized because they are especially tender and flavorful. The major problem is that marcassins happen to be some of the most adorable animals you are ever likely to encounter, with eleven lateral stripes in leafy brown and tan fur. The Japanese call them *uribou* after their watermelon pattern. Marcassins two to three months old, weighing 15 to 20 pounds, can be used for a *rôti à la broche*. This is like roast suckling pig, except that for a suckling pig you must use much more seasoning: marcassin already has a lot of flavor. They must be cooked more slowly, too. At four or five months old, they often require marinades of different sorts. One marinates sanglier to make it tender and less dry, as well as for reasons of taste. There are people who relish the flavor of meat with wine, but Jean-Pierre is different. "It's not bad in my opinion. But it masks the flavor for me. It cuts it. The way that I like marcassin best is in a sauté or a *ragoût*." For this you lightly brown the pieces of meat with butter, oil, and little onions. Add in fermented cider and cook slowly for two or two and a half hours. Put in potatoes; add in a little thyme, bay leaf, salt, pepper, or the mixture known as *quatre épices;* and use some orange or *citron confit,* a kind of salt-pickled lemon, to take away any strong flavor or bitterness in the meat." While Jean-Pierre may not be a big fan of meat marinated in wine, he does enjoy wine with a meal; to accompany boar, he recommends a Burgundy with a little character, such as a Beaune.

In America, the traditional butcher shop that I remember from my childhood has all but disappeared, giving way to prepackaged meat departments at the backs of the aisles in Super Stop & Shops, and the like. The French versions, the *hypermarchés* and *grandes surfaces,* are proliferating both in Paris and in the provinces. Jean-Pierre said that young people aren't interested in becoming butchers, and it is perhaps understandable: "My good friends who are dentists or doctors think I am crazy starting at 4 a.m. and sometimes working until 11 p.m. or midnight. It's not easy to live with people like us."

Despite Jean-Pierre's opinion regarding wine marinade, we decided to use it for our boar just as Madame Delanoe suggested. When Christmas arrived, the loin was taken out of a wine bath seasoned with bay leaves, onion, garlic, rosemary, parsley, and thyme. It was dried, then rubbed with olive oil, and roasted. The marinade was then reduced to deglaze the roasting pan. There was literally no fat to be removed. Mary boiled celery root and made a purée with crème fraîche and nutmeg, and prepared Brussels sprouts with hazelnuts.

Our guests, Mary's French family, arrived and found themselves abruptly seated for Christmas dinner since our cramped flat had little room for much else, particularly when the table was fully extended. The adults started with traditional jade-colored raw oysters, which the children considered nightmarish. They were relieved that smoked salmon could be substituted. The Christmas sanglier followed. It is best served straight from the oven since it tends to lose juices. Despite wild boars being the traditional fare for European celebrations across millennia, our French guests were at once surprised and suspicious. After all, what could we possibly know about cooking boar when most Parisians themselves don't commonly eat it, except perhaps in sausage or pâté? A few tentative bites erased all misgivings, however: the roast exceeded our hopes. The children forgot we were eating the ferocious *bête noire* and simply focused on stuffing themselves.

The night was gusty. I walked the dogs while Christmas lights festooned across the streets and storefronts were swinging about, animated and unruly, a stormy advent of the new year. For many northern cultures, the wild boar served as a symbol of fertility and renewal. The notion of the Christmas pig or boar comes from the fact that formerly every part of the pig was used to supply the family with food for the year — sausages, rillettes, dried haunches, bacon, salted meat, and so on. The fertility of the boar or hog was synonymous with prosperity.

The boar became a symbol of resurrection in Norse culture, and the sacrifice and the splitting of a hog represented Saehrimnir, the cosmic boar who each day was eaten by dead warriors, heroes, and gods only to be found whole again the next day. Our festive roast could not be compared to Valhalla's Saehrimnir, but it was the first of many boar feasts to come. Pursuing the subject of boars illuminated worlds I hardly knew existed, and Frey's golden-bristled boar became a personal metaphor throughout the new year.

Chapter Four

The Beast of Our Emotions

THROUGHOUT THE AGES, wild boars have elicited depictions of ferocity and cruelty that are epitomized by thirteenth-century Franciscan monk Bartholomaeus Anglicus in his bestiary *De proprietatibus rerum* (*On the Order of Things*):

> The boar is so fierce a beast, and also so cruel, that for his fierceness and his cruelness, he despiseth and setteth nought by death, and he reseth full piteously against the point of a spear of the hunter. And though it be so that he be smitten or sticked with a spear through the body, yet for the greater ire and cruelness in heart that he hath, he reseth on his enemy, and taketh comfort and heart and strength for to wreak himself on his adversary with his tusks, and putteth himself in peril of death with a wonder fierceness against the weapon of his enemy.

In one short passage, the monk could hardly have packed more human emotions into one animal. The question is how to reconcile Bartholomaeus Anglicus's description of "wonder fierceness" with what we know about wild boars: they are highly socialized, intelligent animals that prefer to pass their lives peacefully in shadow-filled briar thickets and oak forests, obscured from our mostly diurnal world. Even the males that roam in solitude until rut evaporate at the very hint of human presence. Granted, males will battle each other for mating rights, sometimes with fatal consequences, but boars never attack people unless cornered, wounded, or defending their young.

Still, wild boars offer the ultimate hunting challenge. They are large, powerful adversaries armed with dangerous tusks. Just tracking them can be an ordeal. When finally confronted, boars can summon a brutal charge, even when severely wounded. Because of these challenges, the boar hunt is the stuff of lore: a display of prowess, male rite of passage, whether it is for kings and princes or a bunch of regular guys from our village.

The wild boar has become the beast of our emotions. In a blood drama, it promises to enliven the dullest human heart if it doesn't actually stop it. The boar is anthropomorphized to represent defensive rage and bravery against the gravest odds and thus has been adopted as a military symbol. The animal has served as a military insignia from the time of the Roman legions to the state of Georgia's current Army National Guard. The Polish military named all-terrain personnel carriers and even a submarine after the animal, and the Nazis dubbed their Stuka Thirtieth Fighter Division "The Wild Boar."

Because the progress to the kill remains perilous and volatile, boar hunting can elevate the stature of the boar hunter, in some cases, to mythic proportions. These challenges are portrayed in art: Japanese heroes strangle boars, maharajas slash them with scimitars, Iranian kings shoot them with arrows, imperial English officers pig-stick them with spears, and French nobles run them through with swords. The boar is often portrayed battling unfazed, sporting bright gashes and occupying three men and a host of dogs.

Some works depicting the boar hunt are true masterpieces, capturing the violence, nobility, and pageantry of the kill. Traditions of the boar hunt are represented spectacularly in the calendar series of sixteenth-century Flemish tapestries called the *Hunts of Maximilian* and specifically three tapestries — representing November, December, and January — all concerned with the boar hunt. The tapestries were designed by Bernaert van Orley in 1528–31 and executed in stunning detail by the Dermoyen workshop in Brussels. The scenes woven in silk, wool, and silver- and gold-wrapped thread appear almost three-dimensional. December's *Killing of the Boar,* perhaps the most dramatic in the series, glorifies what is said to be Archduke Maximilian of the Hapsburgs as he thrusts his spear into the massive boar's chest. Hounds cling to the

Raja Jawan Singh of Mewan hunting wild boar, watercolor painting from
Udaipur, 1835. (Photo © Victoria and Albert Museum, London)

boar's ears and ankles in the tumult. Van Orley mastered perspective:
the forest trees appear both near and far, and members of the hunting
party in middle distance, the action converging in the center.

The Spanish master Velázquez's 1630s painting *La Tela Real* offers
the royal spectacle of Philip IV on horseback with his spear extended,
meeting the charge of a wild boar. Unlike Maximilian, Philip is shown
hunting within a huge ring of canvas, keeping the boars from escap-

ing and allowing spectators such as Queen Isabella and First Minister Conde-Duque de Olivares to share the thrill of the king's exploits.

A contemporary of Velázquez, the Flemish painter Frans Snyders essentially created a new genre of painting by producing hyperrealistic renderings of animals and the drama of the hunt. Snyders's work developed during a sudden fascination with the natural world in the Renaissance, and Protestant restrictions on religious imagery led northern European painters to make a striking shift to secular subjects in nature.

In *Wild Boar Hunt,* Snyders captures forces of defense and offense balanced in vicious unresolved action. He shows an enormous boar powering forward with lean, muscular hunting hounds clinging to each ear, while the boar tramples a third that is gripping a jowl. (French hunters use the verb *coiffer* [to dress hair] specifically to describe a boar being taken by the ears, and more generally when the pack hold the animal at bay until the hunters arrive.) Two other hounds have hold of the boar's rear ankles, and two are lying injured on the ground in the lower right of the canvas. More hounds are seen coming as reinforcements from either side of the picture. It is a scene of dogs twisted in every imaginable position, a virtuoso display of hunting-hound anatomy in gymnastic glory.

As in Snyders's tableau, van Orly's tapestry depicts hounds in a boar hunt receiving dreadful wounds. One mounting the back of the boar and catching its right ear is wearing a protective jacket, a precaution used today by some hunters. *La Tela Real,* too, shows boars battling dogs, and there are many other examples even on ancient Greek pottery and in Roman mosaics.

Humans have hunted with dogs from the time they were domesticated from a gray wolf subspecies approximately ten thousand years ago. One can hunt boar from a perch or stalk them or drive them using beaters before a line of shooters: in any case, using dogs is both efficient and traditional. While a broad range of dogs are used in the boar hunt, certain breeds or strains of dogs are effective at tracking a boar, or baying it, or catching it by its snout, ears, tail, or ankles. Boar dogs are highly trained to release their quarry for a clear shot, but the bottom line is that hunting with dogs involves an animal fight that, as an independent spectacle outside of hunting, would in many places be illegal.

Wild Boar Hunt, by Frans Snyders.
(Rockoxhuis Museum, Belgium; © KBC Bank NV, Erwin Donvil)

The beast of our emotions might not be the boar, but our own infatuation with violence, even cruelty. Perhaps Robert Baden-Powell captured this spirit best in his book *Lessons from the Varsity of Life,* in which he defends the sport of pig-sticking in nineteenth-century India: "Try it before you judge. See how the horse enjoys it, see how the boar himself, mad with rage, rushes wholeheartedly into the scrap, see how you, with your temper thoroughly roused, enjoy the opportunity of wreaking it to the full. Yes, hog-hunting is a brutal sport—and yet I loved it, as I loved also the fine old fellow I fought against." Baden-Powell, a founder of scouting for boys, takes Bartholomaeus Anglicus's description of the "wonder fierceness" of boars a step further to include all parties involved. One could easily insert, "see how your dogs cling with rapture."

I remember how crazed the springer spaniel was the first time I saw the two black wild boars, when I blundered into the middle of the hunt. One day I brought our dogs to our country veterinarian of fifteen years, Dr. Françoise Vassallo. By odd coincidence, her clinic shares a common wall with a hunting store stocked with a wide selection of knives, firearms, and ammunition. Dr. Vassallo, a woman of natural sweetness, quick to giggle, was furious with a hunter she'd seen before my appointment. "I just sewed up the same dog with boar tusk wounds that I treated last week," she snapped. "The boar hunts are on Sundays, and hunters find it convenient to bring in their bleeding dogs on Monday."

Dr. Vassallo makes no secret that she's angry about the hunters' mistreatment of dogs, even though being in a hunting zone for sanglier brings in a steady stream of clients. "How many hunting dogs do you treat for wounds?" I asked.

"Last year I sewed up nearly seventy. A number of dogs die on arrival, and, of course, there are uncounted dogs that never make it to the clinic at all." With a little smirk, she added, "A local nurse sewed up the hand of a boar hunter without using any anesthetic. When the hunter queried about a painkiller, the nurse responded, 'Well, you didn't give the boar anesthetic, did you?'"

Dr. Vassallo told us the story of fellow veterinarians whose pet boar had her own couch in the salon and watched television with the family. She assured us that boars are easy to housetrain. I would learn later of the stories of Manni, Max Schnitzel, Wilbur, Arthur, and Ginger, all pet boars.

Even as we were discussing wild boars, Dr. Vassallo received an emergency call from a hunter bringing in a dog with a gashed inner thigh. She explained some of the complications in treating these wounded dogs. "Boars have curved tusks so it's sometimes difficult to follow the line of penetration," she observed. "Organs and vessels can be gravely affected away from the apparent entrance wound. Another problem is that when the chest cavity is punctured, the diaphragm can't produce the suction necessary for respiration, a common problem in treating soldiers on the battlefield. The other dangerous injuries are what you might expect: vital blood vessels severed and ruptured organs."

I asked how common sangliers really were in our area, and she conceded: "It is a *fléau*, a public calamity. There are so many boars that farmers are suffering crop damage. This is why they extend the hunting season here. They start the season in mid-August and extend it sometimes into March, when the sows are already starting to have young."

Everyone I had spoken to about boars confirmed that they present

Feeding time for Ginger, a pet boar. (© John Titchen/Getty Images)

a major problem, justifying culling. There's a general sense that hunt-ers are rendering the country an essential service. Nevertheless, high-priced hunts are also organized at local *domaines de chasse,* enclosed forests that guarantee an even denser population of boar and deer.

My visit with Dr. Vassallo ended abruptly with a buzz at the door and then an importunate knock from the waiting room. "Where should I put him?" the hunter demanded. A champagne-colored griffon Niver-nais sat patiently on the tiles.

"Keep him right there," Dr. Vassallo responded shortly. The blood started to pool. Seeing a real gash rather than one replicated in paint-ings made me queasy as I was leaving. The dog appeared utterly un-perturbed, a tongue lolling out and apparently pleased to be receiving the attention.

While hunting with dogs may be an ancient and noble tradition, many believe it constitutes cruelty to animals. England's recent leg-islation banning the age-old tradition of foxhunting with hounds has ignited a heated debate on what constitutes cruelty to animals. In reply to vociferous antihunting proponents, traditionalists have found veteri-narians to testify that a natural death as a result of disease or famine is crueler than the hunt. Above all, they argue that the legislation turns an age-old class institution into a criminal act and that the law is an infringement on personal freedoms. Inevitably, they point out parallels between the recent interdiction and Nazi-style legislation.

But in fact, Adolf Hitler, a vegetarian, and Hermann Göring, a passionate hunter, enacted some of the most humane hunting laws in Europe. Göring abhorred hunting boar and foxes with dogs, deeming the method cowardly. Legislation against hunting with dogs may have also served as a blow against aristocratic tradition and privilege in the 1930s. Göring's sylvan dream was for Germany to possess the most beautiful, fauna-filled forests in Europe, and to this end he worked not only to protect boars and other game animals but also to introduce exotics, most notoriously raccoons from North America. These have now become such nuisances in Germany that they are called "Nazi raccoons."

A number of northern European countries and some states in the United States have outlawed hunting with dogs, though it's almost impossible to imagine such an interdiction in France. The wild-boar hunt using dogs is considered crueler than a fox hunt because it entails a deadly animal fight in which both boar and dogs suffer injury. At its worst, dog-boar fights have developed into a form of rural entertainment in the American South called hog dogging, hog baiting, hog-dog "rodeos." Feral hogs are not pure Eurasian boars, but they are often mixes of wild boars and fugitive domestic swine. Danielle Ring, in her article "Hog-Dog Fights: Blood 'Sport' Packaged as Family Entertainment," describes a handler prodding a wild hog into a pen with a pit bull:

> And just in case the hog had any notion of trying to defend himself, the handler has already taken the precaution of removing his tusks with bolt cutters.

> The pit bull's owner removes her leash. Before you can count to three-one-thousand, the dog tackles the hog in a cloud of dust. Her jaws tear into the hog's flesh, maybe ripping his snout, tail, or an ear. The hog expresses his pain and fear through loud squeals that echo off the pen's tin walls.

The pit bull's jaws have to be leveraged apart so that the hog can heal up for the next rodeo appearance. The Humane Society may tend toward the hysterical and provide an especially brutal vision of the sport, but the *New Yorker* and the Associated Press have published similar descriptions. An NBC affiliate's investigative coverage of a hog-dog rodeo in Alabama actually led to arrests.

In a real boar hunt, the spectacle is similar, with the important difference that the boar has a fighting chance. Many boars escape wounded. Ideally, hunters train to be good marksmen for efficiency and to minimize an animal's suffering. Boars are notoriously difficult to kill, requiring a coup de grâce — either a well-placed final shot or a fatal jab administered with a specially designed boar knife or long-bladed boar spear. The wounded escapees, however, can take days to die. At one time, tracking them was imperative for sustenance, but these days the practice is a part of the hunting ethic, particularly in nature-loving Germany. Even France can boast of an association devoted to this very purpose: Union Nationale pour l'Utilisation de Chien de Rouge (UNUCR).

A *chien de rouge* is a blood dog, often a teckel or terrier that is a keen scent tracker. Being small, one of these dogs can penetrate thickets and is less likely to alarm an ailing boar than are its larger brethren. Hunters keep a list of certified UNUCR teams in their department and immediately report a wounded boar. The team will set out, sometimes for days, to put a boar or deer out of its misery.

UNUCR hunters take particular satisfaction in their work, and one senses that it's a kind of cult. Their blood dogs compete for distinction in the form of medals and prizes. While there is a high moral imperative, the challenge just to find a suffering animal becomes something of a sport and source of lore in its own right. Stories are swapped and posted on the Internet with a snapshot of the beleaguered beast euthanized and smiling trackers with teckels in one arm and arrows and rifles in the other. Even salvation can be deadly.

Chapter Five

Boars in the Evolutionary Parade

S O WHAT ARE wild boars anyway? This question led me into the fantastical world of taxonomy and an evolutionary parade of peculiar animals, one of which was an entelodont. This distant relative of the wild boar inhabited Europe, Asia, and western North America during the Oligocene and early Miocene periods. Certainly, the term "monster" would fit the rhino-sized omnivore, which stood up to seven feet at the shoulder and sported a three-foot-long head covered with bony protective lumps. An impressive display of enormous teeth completed the terrifying picture. Adrienne Mayor, folklorist and historian of science, dubbed them "Terminator Pigs."

Boars are ungulates, hoofed animals, falling into the order of Artiodactyla — from Greek *artios* (meaning even-numbered) and *dactylos* (meaning finger or toe). In the case of the boar, two-hoofed toes bear weight with two vestigial toes, or spurs, behind them. The Artiodactyla order comprises a great number and range of animals, including pigs, peccaries, hippos, deer, giraffes, camels, antelopes, sheep, goats, and cattle. The boar's suborder, Suiformes, not only includes the entelodont but also has a morphological link to the hippopotamus.

New genetic research has thrown the neatly established order of Artiodactyla into something approaching disarray. The Greeks thought the closest living relative to hippos was the horse, and early taxonomists believed that boars and peccaries were close hippo family members as well, based on molar comparisons. Now scientists are using ever more powerful molecular tools to discover new evolutionary relationships, and thus animal classification is changing. It appears that the Cetacea order — which includes whales and dolphins — are the closest living relatives of the hippo through common ancestry with another extinct piglike animal, anthracotheres. To accommodate these connections, a new branch in the tree of life has been proposed, Cetartiodactyla. Genetic studies have revealed that boars are more distantly linked to hippos than previously thought. Still, I was astonished to learn that boars and entelodonts are linked, albeit remotely, to the truly beautiful monsters, whales and dolphins.

The skeletal structure of an entelodont resembled that of the gift boar I had butchered. The dorsal vertebrae had long spinous processes for supporting huge muscle mass. From the high shoulder, the back tapered, and the neck was short and strong. Like the boar, this animal was designed for power and speed. The appearance of the entelodont and other artiodactyls coincided with major climate shifts that produced extensive grasslands such as the Great Plains of the United States, which favored the survival of fleet mammals suited to the lengthy travel between watering holes.

In the hope of better understanding boar anatomy, I hopped on the line 10 Métro to the Gare d'Austerlitz, just a few steps from the Jardin des Plantes. In the nineteenth century, this was one of Europe's scientific meccas, with museums and research facilities dedicated to biology, botany, geology, mineralogy, zoology, and paleontology.

The zoo that Rilke haunted and that inspired the poems "The Panther" and "The Flamingos" retains its nineteenth-century character: exotic animals behind bars, a barrier through which we can safely ponder wildness. The gardens themselves are a virtual classroom of botany, all plants and trees labeled. One can still feel the presence of Enlightenment thinkers laying the groundwork for the theory of evolution.

Upon entering the Galeries de Paléontologie et d'Anatomie Comparée, which the French poet Paul Celan called the greatest museum in Paris, one is confronted with the monumental sculpture of an ape. Part of its liver hangs out of a wound, and it is strangling a European adventurer while a baby ape watches on. Just a step away, the hall opens onto

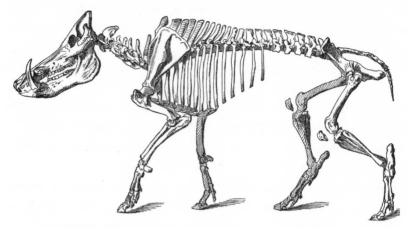

Wild boar skeleton, from Richard Lydekker's *New Natural History*, vol. 2, 1890.

legions of animal skeletons, from delicate, spider web–like bat bones to colossal whale skeletons.

I walked down the left aisle between monkey and panther, then rhinoceros and caribou, arriving at the Artiodactyla display cases: rhinos, hippos, boars, peccaries, deer, and sheep. The paleontology museum seems frozen in time, each specimen identified by a handwritten card, so we are unlikely to see the cases revised to include whales and dolphins.

The wild boar display is not limited to skeletons of our Eurasian variety, *Sus scrofa*, but also includes an array of wild pigs that falls under the Suidae family. One is the warthog with its short snout, wide nostrils, and very long upper tusks curling back like a gigantic ivory-colored moustache. A full warthog skeleton is flanked by a number of skulls. For the children passing the display, the skeleton might evoke the anthropomorphic character Pumbaa in *The Lion King*. Warthogs inhabit the African savannah, and unfortunately for them, hunters covet their tusks as trophies.

Africa has three other suids. The attractive russet-furred red river hogs (African bush pigs), distinguished by long, elegant, pointed ears, live in the humid sub-Saharan forests. The giant forest hog, which is very rare, was discovered only a hundred years ago in Kenya. Scattered colonies exist in African grasslands. More common, at least in Morocco, Algeria, and Tunisia, is the Barbary wild boar, which resembles its European cousins, though perhaps appearing better groomed in consequence of the scarcity of mud.

Male babirusas, a boar relative from Indonesia, sport four long, curved tusks. Two of these curl up from the lower jaw; two others are set peculiarly on the upper surface of the nasal ridge, appearing to curve back into the animal's eyes. While the configuration of tusks provides an inspirational-looking creature for science fiction, scientists have determined that the upper tusks are used for defense and the lower ones for offense. Babirusa means "pig-deer," although the deer association remains a mystery. Unfortunately, as with so many subfamilies of Suidae, the wonderfully weird-looking babirusa is on the brink of extinction.

Its Southeast Asian relative, the bearded pig, is far more numerous. It resembles the gray-furred Barbary boar, except that it has much smaller ears and a pronounced beard around its muzzle.

My favorite of the Suidae family, represented in a full skeleton, is the adorable pygmy hog, found only in the southern Himalayan foothills along the Nepalese-Indian border. This small creature, weighing approximately ten to fifteen pounds and standing less than a foot tall, is so shy, elusive, and scarce that it was thought to be extinct for more than a decade, until in 1971 four showed up in a meat market in northeastern India. They were rescued, triggering a concerted effort to conserve them through breeding and "soft-release" programs. Soft release generally means maintaining animals in a fenced-in and protected habitat, where they can become acclimatized to life in nature before repopulating forested areas.

The second family of wild pigs, Tayassuidae, consists of peccaries. Often called javelinas, peccaries are found in the southwestern United States and throughout Central and South America. There are four species: collared, white-lipped, Chacoan, and giant.

The giant peccary, familiar to locals in the central Amazon forests of

Brazil, first became known to outsiders in 2000, when they were identified by the Dutch eco-hero turned indicted embezzler and bio-thief Marc van Roosmalen, who assisted Lothar Frenz on a nature documentary. He christened the animal *pecari maximus,* a large giant peccary, although it is only the size of a Labrador retriever.

Like the giant peccary, the Chacoan peccary is also a relatively recent discovery. Considered extinct for ten thousand years, the Chacoan was identified only from fossils until the biology professor Ralph M. Wetzel interviewed locals in Paraguay about a mysterious "donkey pig" (named after its donkeylike ears). He finally discovered the animal in 1974 in the dry, scrubby lands of Chaco; later they turned up in Bolivia and Brazil.

Even though the common ancestor of the Eurasian boar and the American peccary existed 40 million years ago and the subspecies developed independently, they share a remarkable number of physical and behavioral characteristics. Most peccaries form a tight matriarchal social structure, are nocturnal, and even have a similar bone to support the rhinal disc for feeding excavations. A group of collared peccaries spotted near Big Bend National Park, for example, would look like a miniaturized version of a compagnie outside of our village.

Texas is at war with feral pigs, whose populations are rampant, and the parks and wildlife services are keen on differentiating them from peccaries. The peccary has three toes on the two hind feet, while the boar has four toes on the hind feet along with other lower leg bone structure variations. The two also have a differing number of teeth, the peccary growing straight canines and the boars curved ones. Peccaries have a complex stomach and no gall bladder, whereas boars possess simple stomachs and gall bladders. Peccaries have notably small tails; boars long, active ones.

Moving clockwise around the great hall of bones, I passed the teratology section displaying genetic and other congenital anomalies expressed as morphological disasters. The animal bodies suspended in formaldehyde-filled cylinders seem specially designed to leave a lifetime scar on the psyches of the child visitor. The Suidae representatives here were a couple of Cyclops pigs and a pig with one head and two bodies.

One entire wall is devoted to the anatomical comparison of organs from different species. Even the most indifferent observer would recognize that the wild boar heart is almost a replica of our own. Perhaps for this reason, the model of the sanglier heart occupies the central position in the heart-model exhibit, flanked left and right by a giraffe heart and a hyena heart, a gorilla heart above it, and a constellation of other animal hearts all about.

The domestication of the wild boar has resulted in the world's number-one source of animal protein despite the fact that large social and religious groups abide by pork consumption taboos. Domesticating the wild boar offered numerous other benefits. As noted previously, the domestic pig's heart is similar to ours in size, general morphology, and function — so much so that it is used in dissection study and surgical practice. The similarity has encouraged medical experts to consider how pig hearts might be used to repair or even replace damaged human hearts. The pig heart-valve transplant has long been an effective treatment for congenital valve problems.

Pig bones have been fitted to human ones in grafts and replacements, and pig skin has helped heal severe burns. Pig insulin is sufficiently close to the human version to be effective in controlling type 1 diabetes, and their enzymes have been modified to fight our diseases. The skin is very similar, susceptible to the same ailments. Less desirably, pigs can act as a mixing vessel for generating new strains of flu viruses. There are far more similarities between swine and ourselves than most people know or would want to believe.

No wonder, then, that biotechnology firms have invested in million-dollar genetically modified pigs in the hope of transforming their bodies into organ-producing farms for curing human diseases. One major step toward this goal would be inactivation of the pig genes that mediate transplant rejection. This use of animal organs, called xenotransplantation, is controversial, and there have been some highly publicized catastrophes, the most notorious being Baby Fae's failed baboon heart transplant in 1984. Concern over the possible creation of catastrophic diseases is legitimate, since the pig is a potential viral pipeline from the animal world to us. Nevertheless, companies contemplate and seek to realize profits in the billions for growing human transplant-compatible kidneys, livers, and hearts in pigs as well as blood suitable for transfusion.

Perhaps the most disturbing consequence of the *Sus scrofa*'s and *Sus domestica*'s physical resemblance to humans is the use of pigs for simulation training in advanced battlefield trauma treatment. A *New York Times* reporter interviewed a U.S. Navy medic in Iraq who described a horrific training exercise in which each corpsman was given an anesthetized pig:

> "The idea is to work with live tissue," he said. "You get a pig and you keep it alive. And every time I did something to help him, they would wound him again. So you see what shock does, and what happens when more wounds are received by a wounded creature."
>
> "My pig?" he said. "They shot him twice in the face with a 9 millimeter pistol, and then six times with an AK-47 and then twice with a 12-gauge shotgun. And then he was set on fire."
>
> "I kept him alive for 15 hours," he said. "That was my pig."

This is not much of an advance over the Middle Ages, when wild boars provided human substitutes on which princes and noblemen could hone their martial skills.

After viewing comparative animal and human stomachs, esophagi, and livers, I came to a well-preserved boar brain, somehow expecting that something in its morphology would reveal secrets of the animal's highly touted intelligence. Though the boar shares the same order with buffalo, goats, and deer, its behavior resembles more closely that of wolves. Recent science has developed a hypothesis that the evolution of intelligence is a product of the success of highly socialized animals in natural selection. While most of the analysis has centered on primates, one can see remarkable similarities when comparing the brains of a wolf, a spotted hyena, and boar. The shape and size are roughly the same, and all have deep cortical foldings indicating a density of neurons. It is believed that the social behavior of boars may have facilitated their interactions with Neolithic farmers.

The wild boar's proclivity for rapid reproduction and growth made it an attractive candidate for domestication. In addition, the vast geographic terrain that boars inhabit provided plenty of opportunity for them to interact with humans. It's likely that boars scavenged around Neolithic settlements and fed on scraps offered them.

The boar was the third animal to be domesticated, after wolves and caprines, and the process didn't occur overnight. Rather, domestication spanned centuries and perhaps millennia and occurred in numerous locations from western Europe to Asia. Bone and teeth specimens found in the strata of a unique Neolithic site in Turkey revealed the progression of boar domestication from the ninth to seventh centuries BC. Archaeologists discovered physical differences in intermediaries between domestic and wild pigs.

In *The Variation of Animals and Plants under Domestication*, Darwin described how domestication and breeding changed the morphology of animals. In pigs bred from the European wild boar, he observed the development of a higher, broader skull; the disappearance of bristles; and the shortening of tusks. Differences develop in leg and ear lengths, form of the ribs, coloration and thickness of hair, and body size and structure. Even the young lose their telltale lateral stripes. Many of the morphological changes are attributed to altered feeding habits. Pigs provided with a rich diet were no longer required to plow up the ground and therefore developed shorter, broader skulls and grew bulky, with less height and strength at shoulders.

Unlike other domestic breeds, pigs reassume the phenotype of their "parent stock" if they return to the wild. Darwin observed: "The young . . . reacquire their longitudinal stripes, and the boars invariably reassume their tusks. They revert also in the general shape of their bodies, and in the length of their legs and muzzles, to the state of the wild animal, as might have been expected from the amount of exercise which they are compelled to take in search of food."

It may be that there are no more pure wild boars left because there is two-way traffic: pigs notoriously find their way back into nature while wild boars penetrate the barriers of domestication. In particular, the wild-boar escapees from hunting reserves in the United States breed with fugitive domestic pigs, creating a variegated race of feral hogs numbering in the millions. This crossbreeding occurs naturally and is encouraged in places where free-range farming practices occur. Now the trend away from purebred domestic swine toward a semi-natural animal is gaining advocates. In France, it has been long appreciated that free-range equals flavor.

On coming to the Galeries de Paléontologie et d'Anatomie Comparée, I searched for an entelodont in the Gallery of Vertebrate Paleontology but had no luck finding one. After seeing so many animal skeletons and pickled organs, I decided to extend my stay at the Jardin des Plantes by visiting the Menagerie and communing with living artiodactyls. While *Sus scrofa* was conspicuously absent, *Sus domestica* was represented by two lethargic potbellied hogs next to an enclosure full of frenetic rabbits and guinea pigs. I was delighted to find nearby a group of charcoal gray peccaries busy scouring the worn ground for insects or popcorn. It's hard to resist the urge to pet them, but a sign warns that peccaries bite. One should keep in mind that peccaries are much closer relatives to the entelodont, or "Terminator Pig," than boars.

Chapter Six

Woodsmen and Boars

I ADMIT THAT few things could be more absurd than a middle-aged man being jealous of his own mother who was moving into her late seventies. Surely some would be dismayed that the source of my jealousy was my mother's uncanny luck in seeing boars all the time. Against all reason and financial sense, my mother bought a powder blue sports car. She'd speed on the country roads listening to progressive jazz with the top down and free-spirited wind whipping her long gray hair. She would practically run into boars wherever she went: boars on the way back from the community swimming pool, boars on the way for birthday drinks, boars near the misty canal, boars in the winter wheat, boars on the very edge of our village. I'd seen just two, scrambling for dear life. This had to change.

The Petite Métairie is a pizza-pasta restaurant so well hidden in the woods it's a wonder anyone knows it's there. Despite its name — which means a "small lease farm"— and its Italian fare, it features décors of the American West complete with cowboys and Indians. One picture shows Sitting Bull riding a giant buffalo while knifing it to death. Yellow Christmas lights are permanently strung across the porch, imbuing nearby trees and a mud-hole playground for geese with an ambient glow. One could easily mistake the Petite Métairie for a backwoods barbecue shack, except all the boisterous talk taking place under longhorns and spurs is in French. The fifteen-minute drive to the restaurant offers another spectacle: wild boars, a lot of them.

It wasn't even dusk when boars materialized before my mother, Mary, and me on the drive to the Petite Métairie. A whole compagnie of them filed into full view outside our village near the Étang de la Grande Rue reservoir. They trotted briskly, tails erect, out of the edge of an untilled cornfield. The large female in the lead crossed the rue des Postillons, lieutenant females spaced behind her with young boars and piglets between. They formed a majestic tribe as they crossed the asphalt, leaped the drainage ditch, and traversed another field before dissolving into the understory.

When I returned to the same spot the next day, I found a well-trodden boar run cutting across the road through the fields on both sides. The sod had been freshly tilled. The run led into the woods, where I saw a small, swampy pond with wallows on its muddy edges. Continuing along the rue des Postillons, I discovered more runs with characteristic prints: cloven hoofs with two smaller marks behind each from the vestigial toes. These toes leave a print wider than the front toes, helping to differentiate boar prints from those of a deer.

On our next outing to the Petite Métairie, we scattered a group of four panicked rousses — immature, red-coated boars. They may have gotten separated from the rest of the compagnie, or perhaps had simply formed a band of young male exiles. In a very short time, I'd gone from seeing just two boars in my entire life to expecting an encounter with them any time I felt the yen for pizza.

You can go to zoos or enclosures to see boars, but they are not the same vigorous animals to be found in the wild, with all their nerves and senses on alert. Boars in nature transform the forest, restoring some of its former mystery and unpredictability: the powerful *bête noire* gets the adrenalin flowing. However, catching a glimpse of boars momentarily from a car doesn't measure up to the experience of observing them in their habitat at their chosen time of day. To reach this end, I didn't have a clue where to begin, except to patrol some boar-haunted tract of woods and hope for a little helpful moonlight.

I recounted my boar experiences to a couple of friends, Catherine and Laurent Harvey, and told them of my plan to observe boars in the woods. The Harveys are both hardworking country doctors, deeply committed to nature and natural foods, as well as such traditional pursuits as quilting and carriage driving. In some ways, they reminded me of the earth-loving hippies of my 1960s adolescence. They often organize their vacations around nature and wildlife experiences, from bear watching in Serbia to birding in Africa. Catherine is directly involved in the protection of local endangered species, in particular the ospreys of the Forêt d'Orléans. Among my good friends, they were the ones who most identified with my interest in boars as creatures rather than targets.

The Harveys invited Mary and me to lunch one Saturday, and on arrival we discovered that Roger Ramond, a forestry professor, and his wife, Jeannie, would join us. The Harveys and the Ramonds had just returned from a trip to Poland's forests, some of the oldest in Europe, where, to no one's surprise, they encountered the famously large Polish boars. Despite the vast Polish forests where the boars could thrive in obscurity, they still manage to make a nuisance of themselves. I had just received a postcard from my Polish-American friend Cecilia: "I'm sitting here on Sarah's front porch in the lower Carpathians with a bunch of other people, drinking beer, dusk falling, and we've been noticing these two fires on a far hill we see burning almost every night. Sarah's husband has just told us that one of the village drunks — a woman who meets her lovers in the woods, etc. — is up there burning tires every night because someone pays her to sleep there and keep the wild boars out of their potato field!" While the Harveys didn't have such colorful Polish stories to relate, they did arrange for me to meet Roger, a forest-management expert with a broad network of connections in his field.

Over a lunch that included the testing of some new Polish recipes gleaned during the trip, I recounted my experience with Monsieur Delanoe's wild boar, adding that I wanted to learn more about boars, even go out and commune with them. "Commune" raised eyebrows. "Well, not hang out with them exactly, so much as see them on their terms," I amended.

That very evening, Roger called: "Are you free Sunday night? I've arranged for us to go out on the Schlumberger domain with the *garde forestier,* a friend of mine. He knows the places where we are likely to see boars. Interested?"

The forestry professor had simply taken it on himself to organize an evening with boars. Who could refuse an outing with true woodsmen? Even Mary was thrilled, a surprise given her nasty allergy to mosquitoes, thus a reluctance to walk in the woods. We put off our Paris return.

"It might rain, so bring a hat," Roger warned, adding, "and take binoculars."

While Monsieur Delanoe may have dropped half a boar in my lap, inadvertently triggering my journey into the complex world of boars, the Harveys had bestowed their own sort of gift, our connection with Roger. Roger made it a personal mission to supply me with opportunities to observe boars, regardless of how long it took or how far we would range. A very slender man with dark hair and beard showing minor infiltrations of white hairs, he was soft-spoken, gentle, and passionate about all things natural. I asked Mary, "Do you think these friends are the French version of the 'beautiful people'?" She just nodded. Need I ask?

Roger grew up in the forest, studied forestry, and taught at the Ecole Nationale des Ingénieurs des Travaux des Eaux et Forêts at the Arboretum National des Barres. The arboretum, less than fifteen miles from our village, has a gorgeous collection of trees, but it had suffered recently from egregious funding cutbacks, forcing the school to pack up and move to Nancy. Roger was left to his retirement and the trees to their own devices. With his background, Roger was a perfect guide, a kind of Virgil teaching the nuances and complexities of our local woods.

With the light already fading, the sky a solid gray, we rendezvoused with Roger in Châtillon-Coligny and then drove with him to meet Monsieur Mineau. A drizzle started, making the fields misty, particularly at their tree-lined edges where I was fully expecting to see boars and venturesome fauna. The vast Schlumberger property, one of the largest private landholdings in France, encompassed selectively cut forests, several chateaux, and more than sixty leased farms, terrain that stretched south to the Loire River. The Schlumbergers, originally from Alsace, created one of world's biggest petrochemical companies and established French mining schools while supporting large-scale scientific research.

We drove up to a small, isolated farmhouse surrounded by machine sheds, where Monsieur Mineau was waiting for us. Middle-aged, he was a burly man despite his smallish stature, clad in a woodsman's threadbare green uniform that smelled of smoke and earth. While Mineau's main responsibility was to manage the domain's enormous lumbering operation, a *garde forestier* also looked after the health of the forest: checking for disease and parasites, preventing fires, and managing wildlife, in addition to thwarting poachers.

Mineau had us climb into his mud-splattered Land Rover as if for a safari. The woodsman and the more refined professor shared local forestry gossip, interrupting each other to point out deer, hares, and owls; animals seemingly everywhere. I was so keyed up with anticipation that I kept mistaking bushes for boars.

We stopped at a small field at the edge of a large wooded area with an alley cut through it. We stole across the field as quietly as we could, forewarned that even the rustling of fabric will alarm boars. We took up our station at the entrance to the alley and waited for boars to appear. The light lingered, but the rain increased while we stared into the trees and listened to the drops in the leaves. I hadn't practiced that sort of silence since I was a kid: standing still in nature for an hour and a half without a word or a whisper, opening the senses — the simplest sort of mysticism, really.

The Schlumbergers' property was anything but wilderness, however: distant aircraft passed overhead, the steady traffic whined on the country roads, and dog barks reached us from a farmhouse. What actually constitutes the peace of the forest? Perhaps it didn't exist at all in France. Or rather what we experienced now was it. Roger told us boars were entirely habituated to the rumble of human commerce around them.

Rain was dripping off our caps, and from time to time Roger gestured silently, indicating the direction of animal movements. I couldn't distinguish them from the sound of the rain, or of leaves flickering in the breeze. I'd stare down the alley with binoculars for a steady ten minutes at a time, the branches forming a tunnel of darkness with a luminous opening at the far end in which I expected to see boar silhouettes appear. Monsieur Mineau and Roger signaled more movement, cracked twigs, shuffling, then nothing.

Dusk had given over to full dark, and we all knew our chances of seeing a boar were over. Anticipation melted into the relaxed pleasure of watching the night rain. Then, suddenly a quick rustling set our hearts pounding. An animal was moving through brush straight toward us. As it closed in, I entertained visions of a boar bursting out of the bushes. Aren't they supposed to evade humans? Instead of a boar, though, a young roe deer stepped in front of us, with an expression of startled disbelief. Having stumbled upon dangerous company, she vanished into the underbrush.

Monsieur Mineau declared the boar watch over, but he kindly took us out in the Land Rover along the rutted forest tracks. There we saw plenty of boars — groups of two or four fleeing the headlights — but no compagnie or large males. Our inability to stalk boars successfully on foot was unacceptable to the foresters, and boar-observing plans were made for the following weekend.

On the second expedition, Mineau drove us to a different area on an overcast, humid evening with no rain. We entered dense woods off a farm tract and soon encountered a half-drained, fetid pond with a green slick on the surface and fallen trees rotting along the edges. Boar tracks littered the muddy banks, and at least seven pits had been dug to form the sloppily contoured wallows that boars adore. With branches in our faces and darkness coming on, we stumbled our way over abandoned wire fencing, small stone walls, and ditches to the far end of the pond, stopping on a ledge where we could use low branches as camouflage. Standing just inches from each other, the four of us fell silent, staring at a corridor to the pond, taking in leaf odors and the pinkish hue of the clouds above the trees.

The woods crackled with animal sounds. Roger squeezed my shoulder every few minutes and would put his forefinger to his ear and then point to a place in the woods where we could hear treading in the leaves, snapping twigs, and hog noises. There was no question that we were in the presence of boars this time, and we heard one cautiously approaching. Suddenly two loud teals whistled out of the sky between the trees and splashed down into the pond, quacking volubly. More ducks followed, dropped through the branches, and as soon as they crashed into the pond they started to squabble.

So much for the boar, we thought; but after a pause the hesitant movements in the woods resumed. Finally, a single large animal loomed in front of us. I could hear it scratching itself on oak bark; I could see the tree. Mary suddenly spied it, and Roger tapped my shoulder and pointed. I heard the boar shamble from the oak to the water's edge, where it drank. But, instead of sliding down into the mud, as we all anticipated, the animal turned and retreated into the woods.

Roger was forced to break silence: "Do you see it? It's a very large male." Mary nodded. Monsieur Mineau and Roger were thrilled: they had brought us to a magnificent boar. I received a satisfied pat on the back, as though I had fetched it myself.

I'd been looking right at the animal, or the spot where I heard its unmistakable movements. But something was wrong with my angle of view, an obscuring branch perhaps. It was already dark, and I couldn't verify what I saw. Roger sensed this. He and Mineau grew quiet. What in the world did they have to do? No one could possibly have missed a boar so large.

"Maybe it's better to look for boars in winter in moonlight," Mary offered. "There are no leaves, and the nights are longer." She turned to Mineau and asked, "Can we come here on our own?"

"No," he responded brusquely. We were on private land, and he couldn't take responsibility for accidents caused by boars or hunters. His job was to keep an eye out for trespassers and poachers. We thanked Mineau profusely nonetheless and rode back to our car with a rather pensive Roger.

Later, I asked Mary, "What did you see?"

"Well, first there was rustling, grunts, and snorts. Then a gray shadow appeared, and it scratched itself, and then it left."

"Was it big?"

"The gray shadow? Yes, well, Roger and Mineau said it was big, so I thought so too."

Was this gray shadow really the same animal to which Bartholomaeus Anglicus in *On the Order of Things* applied the words "cruel" and "fierce"? For him, the wild boar was the beast of our most extreme emotions, and even Monsieur Mineau claimed that a "ferocious" compagnie of boars had once sent him scrambling up a tree. Still, Mary's vision stuck with me — a scene of boars, their soft, ambiguous figures rooting peacefully among the moonlit trees.

Our boar expeditions had opened up the world of foresters to us. It was easy to admire the lives they'd chosen. They were managers; they shaped the woods and thus were part of them. Controlled cutting provided renewable energy while maintaining a healthy forest. The profession fit the romantic vision of human beings in balance with nature; a mutual nurturing.

Through Roger and Mineau, I learned of a very specialized sort of woodsman, one who held a public office through expertise in both forestry and hunting: the *lieutenant de louveterie*. Literally, the title means "officer of wolf catching." It's an ancient and honored position, an office created by Charlemagne in 812. At the king's court, the *louvetier royal*, the Wolf Catcher Royal, commanded lieutenants, *sous-lieutenants*, huntsmen, and dog-handling valets assigned to particular breeds and hunting methods. While the *louvetier* and his men assisted in royal hunts, his primary duty was to protect livestock from wolves, the peasants being in no position legally or materially to cope with wolves themselves. Like Monsieur Mineau, the *louvetier* also policed the forests against poachers. Shortly after the Revolution, this royal position was dissolved along with Ancien Régime, but it was quickly reinstated as a result of the urgent need for knowledgeable forest officers.

At a local newspaper store that sold a few eclectic paperbacks, I bought *La chasse au sanglier en Puisaye,* by Jean Lavollée, a contemporary *lieutenant de louveterie* in our region, whose father had held the same position before him. The book provides a personalized history of boar hunting from the nineteenth century to the present in the Puisaye. It also tracks boar populations in our region going back to the Revolution. Lavollée contends that our area didn't experience significant agricultural damage from boars because wolves controlled their populations through the entire nineteenth century. Wolves, like boars, possess keen senses and are difficult to hunt without trained dogs to track them down and bay them.

With the eradication of wolves in France in the early twentieth century, the *lieutenants de louveterie* and their dogs inherited a new responsibility — ironically of their own making — controlling the soaring boar populations. A wolf can consume forty or more wild boars annually, mostly the young or sick ones: wolves are unlikely to tangle with a mature male or a tough female. The *lieutenants de louveterie* retained their honored title by way of French tradition, though the designation had become obsolete.

One of the main responsibilities of the *louvetier* these days is to organize communities to execute battues officially ordered by local authorities to reduce crop damage. A battue is a hunting method dating back to Paleolithic times, perhaps earlier, where lines of *rabatteurs,* or beaters, would systematically thrash their way noisily through underbrush to drive wild animals into traps, off of cliffs, or in front of a group of shooters. The tricky part is silently setting up the *rabatteurs* with their sticks, pipes, drums, and dogs on three sides of a forested area and then positioning shooters so as to limit the danger of losing dogs and comrades to friendly fire. Interestingly, some scholars have used the organization of the battue as a model for primitive notions of communism, since community members of varying ages and both sexes can participate for the greater good of all.

According to Lavollée, the first major surge in local boar populations occurred during the Great War. Many believe wild boars fled the large armies and artillery and machine-gun fire that ripped through the

"Capturing Wild Boars Feeding in Fields and Orchards,"
Gaston Phoebus illustration from 1407 edition of *Livre de la chasse*.
(The Pierpont Morgan Library, New York; Bequest of
Clara S. Peck, 1983; MS M.1044, fol. 96v)

Ardennes forests. Wild boars allegedly ranged south as far as the Loire River and beyond since rivers were no impediment to boars. Populations rose again during the Second World War. Lavollée attributes this to the World War I depletion of men as well as to the fact that hunting and possession of firearms were prohibited during World War II in occupied northern France.

With boars causing considerable damage during World War II, Lavollée's father, Ernest, organized battues under the supervision of three or four German officers, who would join the firing line. The *lieutenant de louveterie* was responsible for distributing and collecting firearms, but could not apportion the meat. The German officers selected the choicest quarry.

Lavollée relates that the Germans ordered a surprise battue in forest areas and thickets north of our village where they believed members of the eponymous resistance hid. A larger contingent of thirty soldiers suddenly joined the firing line and the *rabatteurs*. Thus, in a sense, Ernest Lavollée and the locals participated as hostages in a manhunt for their own neighbors.

Recently the *lieutenants de louveterie* have been showing up in the news. The forest experts have adapted their battues to urban conditions as expanding boar populations are pushing toward cities and the suburbs. Even our trips to the Petite Métairie take us across disputed land. Landowners complain about the enormous boar population while the hunters want it that way, as had the royalty of France, the guarantee of a fruitful hunt. Now chateau grounds and the woods of Europe have become managed parks with unmanageable boars. The remnants of true wilderness, it appears, are moving in with us.

Chapter Seven

The Noble Domain

FIRST VISITED THE Château de Chambord some twenty years ago during the most frigid winter we'd ever lived through in France. Built on flat land and surrounded by an enormous forested park within the larger Forêt Domaniale de Boulogne, the chateau emerges suddenly in an open field, one astonishing building producing a dreamlike cityscape in winter silence. Integrating medieval and Renaissance architecture, the chateau was meant to evoke a utopian ideal, a model of a "celestial Jerusalem" or Constantinople. A medley of monumental turrets, elaborate chimneys resembling towers, conical and pitched roofs, large windows, ramparts, terraces, and staircases conspire to produce this hallucinatory effect.

For all its splendor, Chambord served merely as a grandiose hunting lodge, and it remains a consummate symbol of European royal privilege and extravagance. And yet Chambord's story over the centuries has been one largely of neglect and abandonment. Now, its true glory has never been greater than it is in the twenty-first century. Nearly 2 million people visit it annually.

Near the entrance to the park, images of a deer and a wild boar in profile warn that large animals are *en liberté*. Each year, dozens of automobilists pay a price for taking this intelligence too lightly. On our first trip to Chambord, my mother, Mary, and I stayed at the Saint-Michel, a former dog kennel transformed into a two-story hotel. It might be hard to believe that a hotel with a good-sized restaurant would be fashioned from a dog kennel, but considering that the stables housed up to

1,200 horses, the kennel was consistent with Chambord's preposterous dimensions.

That first evening, I walked my mother's golden retriever, Angel, across the bridge over the frozen Cosson River, which bisects the park, and then onto a path among the black trees. I was confident that large animals would emerge in these openings. Certainly wild boars were beginning their nocturnal stirrings and break cover, but no such luck. Even with the great density of animals on the domain, the only movement we would see was the swirl of snow.

Ever since that first visit, I have regularly seized excuses to return to Chambord, mainly bringing friends. It is the largest of the Loire Valley chateaux and one of the most extravagant in the world, with 440 rooms, 84 staircases, and 365 fireplaces. Apparently hoping to be nearer his mistress, the Comtesse de Thoury, François I had the chateau constructed between 1519 and 1547, creating an architectural symbol of his own majestic stature. François I was so ambitious for his project that he even contemplated directing the Loire River to the chateau, allowing ships to pass its splendor.

Paradoxically, as construction was getting under way, François I diverted royal power to Paris and the Île-de-France area, shifting focus away from the Loire Valley, where he had already contributed to the construction and renovation of a number of the chateaux. It also became clear that a residence of Chambord's proportions was impractical, being too far from sufficient food and supply resources to support the enormous royal entourage and staff.

François I personally laid out Chambord's first royal hunting ground, ordering the acquisition of lands that included forests, marshes, ponds, thickets, meadows, and farms. These grounds would be dedicated to the conservation of the land itself and to safeguard the "red and black beasts" (as he referred to deer and boars) for the pleasure of hunting them.

Several decades later, Charles V doubled the area and had a twenty-two-mile-long wall erected, encircling an area larger than the city of Paris. Such grounds for conserving game and ensuring aristocratic

Wild boar with red deer. (© Laszlo Balogh/Reuters)

hunting amusement were typically associated with sixteenth-century French chateaux, such as Fontainebleau, which Francois I vastly transformed and expanded, and Rambouillet, where the great hunter/builder king died. A century after work started on Chambord, Louis XIII ordered the initial construction of a hunting lodge that would eventually become the vast Château de Versailles, its highly formal grounds meant to symbolize man's "tyranny over nature."

With the Revolution and historical upheavals, all of these chateaux experienced the vagaries of neglect and revitalization. Just after World War II, the domain of the Château de Chambord was decreed the presidential hunting reserve. Besides serving the French president and various dignitaries for ceremonial hunts, the reserve was dedicated to animal conservation, experimentation in forest management, and environmental education. Of the larger animals at Chambord, wild boars are the most populous and prolific, requiring systematic culling. Large deer are raised, captured, and so broadly distributed in various forests in France that 60 percent of the stags have bloodlines traceable to Chambord. In addition, the endangered Corsican mouflon (wild mountain sheep) are raised and introduced into appropriate habitats.

The stag has always been considered the most noble and therefore prized animal at Chambord, coming to symbolize the chateau itself along with the ubiquitous salamander motif on the king's coat of arms. Attitudes toward the boar, on the other hand, varied radically in the world of European elites, depending on the particular personalities of the noblemen or on local traditions.

Sixteenth-century kings and princes in France hunted as a display of privilege, pleasure, and pageantry rather than for sustenance. One can imagine the hunt as a panoramic spectacle observed at a distance from the chateau terraces — princes on horses, valets and huntsmen in attendance, and dogs swarming stags. At Chambord, the boar was mostly shunned, particularly by the princes of Bourbon-Parma, yet few hunted animals could duel like a boar. Often the boar hunt became a kind of military exercise for nobles, and one can easily see the appeal to the hot-blooded Maréchal de Saxe, on whom Louis XV conferred Chambord for his brilliant military exploits against the Duke of Cumberland at the Battle of Fontenoy. The maréchal took particular delight in driving stakes through netted wild boars in his waning years, when he was nearly immobile with edema, and had to be carted in a chair to avail himself of this violent pleasure.

While the boar may never enjoy the romantic status of the great ten-pointed stag at Chambord, it has clearly become the dominant animal, as it has at almost all other French chateau estates. Many are bred specifically to supply much-need hunting income as a means of offsetting the high cost of preserving the centuries-old edifices.

One hot afternoon in late spring, I set out by myself for the Château de Chambord with the express purpose of sighting a wild boar. We were staying with friends at their country house on the Cher River where it passes through the Loire Valley. This region is known as the Sologne, just west of our Puisaye in Bourgogne. Flat land with large forests between the Loire and Cher, the Sologne features numerous rivers with marshes, ponds, and tributaries formed over an impermeable base of clay and sand. The area was known long before the construction of Chambord for its wealth of fauna and game, and hunting reserves and selective lumber cutting remain a significant source of income.

Chambord maintains a population of nearly one thousand wild boars, of which five hundred are culled during hunting season. Along two of the limited public routes, wildlife observation decks have been erected recently, allowing visitors to peer out across meadows and into forested lands that are otherwise off-limits. When I expressed the hope that as the afternoon wore on I might spot some boars, my friends were dubious. "I have never seen a boar at Chambord," one cautioned. "Good God," sniffed another. "Why boars?"

I discovered two miradors, Ricanère and Rond Béatrix, somber wooden structures with lowbrow roofs, Spartan benches, and ledges for discreetly posing cameras and telescopes. They had been positioned a little more than a half mile apart and rose over hedges and fencing, allowing nature enthusiasts to scan the grasses and shrubs along the edges of denser woodlands. Inside the mirador, the imposed silence is reminiscent of a forward military surveillance post. Encouragingly, boars had excavated both roadside shoulders and broad areas around the miradors.

I admit to idealizing the kind of patience it takes to observe wildlife. It requires a disciplined attentiveness, a pleasant Zen-like way out of self-absorption into the act of noticing. Still, given the challenge of observing wild boars, one learns more about tolerance for frustration or boredom. It is said that when alarmed, even the heaviest wild boars can move over dead leaves more quietly than a blackbird.

I imagined that observing animals at France's most famous nature preserve would be like canned hunting. There is no mystery about where the animals are; they are walled in just as they once were for ease of dispatch by noblemen. You simply have to go to them. Several hours of peering into the forest and tallying a wildlife count of a few common birds made it clear how wrong I was. Moreover, tourist buses and steady traffic destroyed any hope of an Emersonian epiphany in nature.

Still, wild boars had indisputably dug up the grounds around the wildlife observatories. The surface detritus had been cleared in areas of more than fifty feet of forest floor, exposing roots and creating shallow pits, a boar version of strip mining. Hoof prints were ubiquitous, and tree trunks showed telltale signs of rubbing. I followed the fencing that delineated the narrow lanes of public land from the restricted reserve. I had hardly progressed more than a few hundred feet before flies began to swarm me. Having lived near pastures and experienced similar on-slaughts, I knew large animals were near. Within moments, a boar ap-peared in the understory — black bristled with massive shoulders; the healthy bulk of his tapered body; soft, almost fluffy ears aloft, attentive; and small, watchful eyes. Strong and full-tusked, he was exactly the beautiful monster I had hoped to see. And, yes, he moved making less leaf noise than a hopping blackbird.

Not content to appreciate the moment and remain quiet, I clumsily tried to stalk the boar with a pocket camera and managed to catch up with him three times. Then he simply slipped through a hole in the fencing to vanish into thick brush. This was the first boar that I had unquestionably encountered on foot, a magnificent creature that ap-peared powerful, yet I never felt threatened. Looking at the gaping hole where I lost him, I could see that the fence served more to keep people out than hold animals in. After all, a boar my size, or larger, had been on my side of the fence.

Before I had much time to reflect on my good fortune, another boar appeared on my right, smaller, but more mature than a year-old *bête rousse*. Its blackish coloration resembled that of the male I'd just seen, but this boar had yet to acquire the same bulk, and though it lingered, it maintained a greater distance. I couldn't tell whether it was male or female. This second boar was far less skittish than the first, stopping to root around the base of young oaks. When I tried to close the gap between us, however, it moved off toward the cover of shrubs and low branches.

"Good God, why boars?" Well, because they're exciting. On this sin-gular point, Maréchal de Saxe would agree, if he could see me across the ages trespassing on his land. Monsieur Olivier, the hunter–nature artist, would call it "passion." With the lynx, wolf, and bear eradicated or marginalized to the most remote of areas, the wild boar is truly the king of the forests.

As evening set in, I returned to the chateau to pick up some information on the park. I had noticed a major shift in Chambord's public face. Many of the banners hanging near the concession stands, and the ticket office depicted the animal life of the park, and wild boars and deer in particular. Among the shows and activities — including the nocturnal "Dream of Lights," the Renaissance Ball, the equestrian spectacle, the grand concert of hunting trumpets, and the nights of *brame* (belling of stags) — Chambord offered four-wheel drive "safari" treks on the reserve specifically to see wildlife. François I's fantasy world had devolved into an ecotourism destination.

By the time I was able to report to Roger that I had at last met up with wild boars while on foot (supported by photos of shadowy indistinguishable forms), he had already arranged for me to meet his longtime colleague Francis Forget. Monsieur Forget, trained as a water and forestry engineer, had devoted his entire professional life to the management of the Chambord domain. He served as the director of the reserve for fifteen years before being named director of the patrimoines and counselor for hunting and forestry, a position he holds even in retirement. For decades he organized the presidential hunts, and on occasion Roger and his students assisted. Many of the chateau's official book and banner photographs, including those of the animals on the reserve, turned out to be Monsieur Forget's. Out of his life-long devotion to forestry and so many years of administering the domain and hunts, he had developed a passion for photography, and his images are now a part of the Chambord legacy.

Roger had arranged for us to meet Monsieur Forget on the patio in front of the Saint-Michel. Twenty years had passed since I had first stayed at the dog kennel cum hotel: now I was back, but this time for a personal tour of the presidential hunting reserve and some serious boar-spotting. There could hardly be a greater contrast between my first visit on a frigid January night and this one on a brilliant day in May, the grounds streaming with tourists, including Russians and eastern Europeans, rare in the past.

The clean-cut Monsieur Forget was seated in the sun talking to colleagues when we arrived. He didn't seem old enough for retirement: he had the healthy mien of a forester but the decorum of an administrator, and indeed he was still very active. After cordial introductions, Forget began to describe the administrative headaches he had experienced at Chambord, beginning with the early 1980s and the Socialist administration of François Mitterrand. Before 2005, he told us, Chambord had been run by three public establishments: the Forestry Office, the Office of Hunting, and the Center for National Monuments. Officials from the Army, Republican Guard, Culture, Agriculture, and Environment also contributed to the administration of Chambord. Even the Ministry of the Interior played a role because the 220 inhabitants of the village of Chambord rented from the French state.

President Pompidou, who loved Chambord ("a coup de foudre," said Francis), created the administrative structure in 1969 because the chateau and its grounds had been so poorly managed and maintained. Now, thirty years later, the administration has been restructured. "One no longer speaks of just the forest and the chateau," Francis observed, "but also of heritage and welcoming the public."

This, then, accounted for the extraordinary transformation at Chambord that I had noticed. While the bureaucracy may have produced headaches, Pompidou was a visionary, determined to make Chambord a center devoted to nature, hunting, and culture. He enlisted the industrialist and patron François Summer to attract the public to the reserve and create the Museum of Hunting and Nature. "Chambord's identity is based on a hunting territory and a chateau," Francis continued. "A combination like this has become very rare since the beginning of the last century. Chambord is perhaps the sole example in France or even Europe of an attempt to preserve this dual historical identity — a hunting park within walled grounds and a great chateau. Fontainebleau and Rambouillet have forests, but the original hunting parks no longer exist."

Even in semi-retirement, Francis remained a passionate ambassador for Chambord, emphasizing its uniqueness. He still scheduled state hunts, welcomed hunters, and coordinated the *battue de prestige* for wild boars and deer. The *battue de prestige* includes all the trappings and traditions of an organized formal hunt: the beaters in red vests, dog handlers in green vests, trained fox terriers. The Garde Républicaine often gives a hunting-trumpet concert, and all the invited participants enjoy excellent meals with fine wines.

Francis listened politely to my description of how wild boars had captivated my attention, and of my boar-watching nights with Roger and Monsieur Mineau. I lamented the difficulty of encountering a boar, or even getting a momentary glimpse of one. Roger raised the possibility that we might not see one today. "The last time we came with a busload of foresters from the arboretum, we spent the day at Chambord without seeing a single boar," he sighed.

"You can't predict. We may see none." Francis agreed. "The chances are better at night."

Francis pulled out a map and showed how circumscribed the public portion of the park was. The vast chateau appeared as a negligible inch-long rectangle in the midst of concentric parks of Chambord within Boulogne. He pointed out the specified routes that bicycles, horse-drawn carriages, and four-wheel drive vehicles follow. One area was designated for teaching biology and forestry; another for *chasse photographique* limited to only two photographers a day during two months of the year. Meanwhile, almost the entire reserve was still used for real hunting, the exception being those areas where public safety might be compromised.

In contrast to our first wild-boar safari in a mud-splashed military green, hard-suspension, four-wheel-drive vehicle, Francis fetched his spotless white sedan, and we drove to a gate north of the chateau near the Faisanderie de la Peverie, an aviary for raising pheasants and other game fowl. As one would expect in a chateau forest extending over flat ground, all the roads and alleys were cut in straight lines. We scanned the woods, the oaks with new green leaves; the grasses sprouting and ferns freshly unfurled. Once again, it was Roger who began spotting boars. He had an uncanny ability to discern movement and form when most people would see static stumps and rocks.

"Look: go back, go back!" he abruptly ordered Francis, who immediately stopped and reversed to an alley.

"Where's your camera?" he hissed at me urgently.

I did see the two boars dashing out of the ferns, but what I managed to get a photo of was a car window framing an empty alley. We repeated this same exercise — of dashing boars and subsequent photographs of the dashboard and the backs of my companions' heads — twice more before arriving at a compound of five former farm buildings called La Guillonnière.

Meadows border the old farm except where a shallow pond flanks the western side. We parked between the buildings, two of which featured camouflaged miradors, giving them the appearance of farmhouse gun emplacements left over from World War II. I stepped out of the car and looked over the fence into the south meadow where, as if conjured up by Francis, a compagnie of boars was peacefully working the earth. I began frantically pointing, but Francis grabbed my arm, and with a finger to his lips led us into the small house and up the wooden stairs to the mirador, where we observed the boars for ten minutes through the camouflage netting.

The young gamboled about the feet of the females. One moment the sows appeared utterly relaxed, swishing their tails, poking and rooting; the next moment they'd freeze in vigilance, ears erect, tails rigid. Then, resuming their foraging, they crossed the meadow in profile, charcoal against the vivid green grasses, toward a lone apple tree. When a noisy magpie flew into the tree, the entire group bolted ten yards and stopped, statuesque, the large females in front. Each member of the compagnie was wired to a single common nerve. When the alarm subsided, the group carried on digging and frolicking until they finally disappeared from view, blending into the forest cover.

Even Francis and Roger, who had seen hundreds of wild boars, both alive and dead, over the years, seemed gratified. Somehow it never grows old, discovering these majestic animals. The marcassins appeared comically rough-and-tumble, pouncing on top of each other, pushing one another around. It was May, their time.

Afterward, Francis gave us a tour of La Guillonnière. Two of the farmhouses served as both animal observatories and dormitories. The small pond provided a watering place for birds and four-legged beasts and a wallow for muck-loving boars. A central building was used as a conference area for wildlife education, public visits, and park hunting and conservation planning. This building had been transformed into a shrine to boars. The compagnie that we had just observed seemed replicated in a taxidermy display — sows and squeakers in natural parade across the west wall. On each wall, boar heads, some mounted with their erstwhile owner's forefeet, stared in, and the mounted head of a great white boar presided over all. Boar skeletons were on display, as were jaws demonstrating the wear of maturation and aging on the teeth. Dozens of trophy plaques with cutters and whetters mounted in a series of crescents lining the walls just below the ceiling, each plaque bearing a small bronze plate etched with the date of the kill.

Up in the mezzanine between the bones and the heads, photographs showed the boars both in nature and the battue, some photographed at the very moment a bullet tore through them. Another showed a young boar contentedly gnawing on an antler. Many captured the ceremonial display of the quarry, boar carcasses symmetrically arranged in rows, at the feet of the men who hunted them. This was an archetypal image I'd see again and again on cell phones, on walls, on the Internet. One photograph showed a beater balancing himself on his stick with his pants pulled down below his knees. A lightninglike red gash ran the length of his inner thigh. The odd little hall dedicated to the boar reminded me of Olivier's art studio: it was worshipful in some essential human way.

As we made our way through the park, we continued to encounter small groups of boars with their young, sometimes a single laie with marcassins. By the end of the trip, Roger asked, "How many boars do think we've seen?"

"Maybe twenty or even twenty-five," I hazarded.

"I counted twenty-nine."

"We were unusually fortunate today," Francis confirmed. It never occurred to me to count the boars, but maybe it was a naturalist's habit.

After a pause, Francis said, "If you want to participate in the presidential hunt, write a formal request to me and we can work you in."

"That is extremely kind."

Roger intruded, sensing my nature: "I don't think you'd enjoy it. It's bloody."

A month later I read that Chambord was holding its annual two-day Game Fair. On a whim, I drove from Rogny on the Sunday and arrived in time for a formal hunting-horn concert and a peculiar hunters' mass in which the unexpected theme was the bravery and suffering of the Jewish people. Hunting-dog competitions were being held. I visited each team's kennel, many sporting mounted boar heads or photos of boars. Constant gunfire could be heard from the woods, where gun sellers had set up eight trap-shooting stands, all in simultaneous use. I strolled through the crowd of vendors selling every possible hunting item: exquisitely crafted guns; gorgeous breeds of tracking, baying, and catching dogs; and excursions for hunting exotic animals in extreme parts of the planet.

On the way out, I visited the Museum of Hunting and Nature, envisioned by President Pompidou and executed by François Summer on the chateau's second floor. There I was astonished to find the "January" tapestry from the *Hunts of Maximilian* on display from Beaux-Arts de Chartres. Apparently, the Dermoyen weaving workshops in Brussels made editions of Orley's sixteenth-century masterpieces, all twelve of which are exhibited in their cinematic glory at the Louvre. While December might be the most dramatic scene of Hapsburg Archduke Maximilian driving a spear into a boar in the Belgian Forest of Soignes, January's *La Curée d'un sanglier* is technically one of the most remarkable. The tapestry portrays the precisely codified ritual of the cleaning of the boar, which includes presenting the head, fierce jaws held open with a baton, to the master of the hunt, who is portrayed on horseback. A panel explains that the ritual includes feeding entrails mixed with bread to the hounds, some of which are shown still cloaked in their protective jackets. At the center of the scene, the headless carcass of the boar, bristles and all, is set over a blaze on a spit, tended by valets.

How did the weavers create such panoramic realism out of hachures of wool, gold, and silver? The loom work coalesces into flame and smoke rising, the smoke-veiled chateau in the distance, the illuminated sky and the shadows under men and dogs, boars strung by their hooves. The Archduke Maximilian was a contemporary of François I, and the tapestry a breathtaking vision of their time.

Chapter Eight

Nights in the Forest

TWO ROUSSES, females, spotted me from a managed copse on the far side of a broad fallow field. To my surprise, instead of fleeing or receding into the trees, they came trotting straight over to greet me at a fence. They paused and lifted their snouts in an inquisitive fashion, taking a few exploratory sniffs. Their eyes were smallish but gentle, framed by long, soft lashes. One boar looked as if she'd visited the coiffure for a frost job; light, almost silvery bristles were streaked over dark brown fur.

What did I have in the car to give them? Tic Tacs? Lemon drops? Stale potato chips?

The rest of the compagnie, twenty-one boars altogether, finally lifted their snouts from the never-ending business of ravaging the sod and took notice of me. Then they, too, crossed the field, but at a more leisurely pace. The young ones, with their vivid stripes, bounded along, often stumbling over each other, sometimes breaking into a comical piglet gallop. All arrived milling about and sniffing, but the dominant sow turned impatient, then suspicious. She gave me a short, searching stare, grunted dismissively, and wandered off. The others followed her lead, some rooting as they went, others just roughhousing.

Each time I come to the Domaine de Tombereau, I look for boars. They are raised for the specific purpose of stocking the woods, where, one Sunday in autumn or winter, they will be shot down. The hunting domain is south of us, not far from the village of La Bussière, home to a picturesque private chateau on a lake. Essentially an aristocratic fishing lodge, it is endowed with an elaborate eighteenth-century kitchen garden that draws tourists from near and far.

Usually at the Domaine de Tombereau, herds of deer are more visible than boars, but the proprietor shifts the enclosures every year or two — the animal version of crop rotation — and leaves fields to recover from grazing and rooting. The boars had been turned out on a field close to the road, so I was able to get close to them without trespassing. They weren't always visible, but whenever I saw them in passing I'd pull over on the brink of a drainage ditch. The same young females usually rushed to greet me, but sometimes different, even younger boars would show up.

I soon noticed that boars had also churned up large stretches of sod on both sides of the fence, meaning that wild boars were filtering out of the woods to hold midnight meetings with the enclosed boars. The fence delineated their two modes of behavior: one group curious and even friendly; the other elusive and vigilant. The animals outside the fence, outlaws and highly valued as game, couldn't afford to be curious about humans.

Oddly, the wild boars had to follow the road that made a corridor between the two fences in order to mingle with their captive cousins. In a country devoid of wilderness, all boars are penned up to varying degrees, if not by actual fences then by highways and walls. The highway system itself alone is a vast matrix of barriers, mitigated somewhat by wild-animal bridges with blinds on each side and by animal underpasses beneath raised roadways. Both are disguised with weeds, brush, and trees. The French joke that hunters stake out these passages, and who knows? Maybe they do. In any case, it's hard not to see the fence between the wild and the captive boars as a symbol of our relationship with them. We touch them, we fence them in, and then they lose their spirit and become dependent. The sense of wilderness vanishes in the animal. All the same, they become endearing.

To the outrage of his English farming neighbors, the staunch vegetarian rock legend Paul McCartney refuses to cull wild boars on his 1,500-acre Peasmash property in East Sussex. The possibility for such a

English lady and a boar. (© David J. Slater, djsphotography.co.uk)

conflict didn't exist in England until the past decade. In England, indigenous boars were rendered extinct in the thirteenth century, and then killed off again after a brief reintroduction for noble hunting recreation. However, efforts to reintroduce boars continued through subsequent centuries. Now, thanks to regular escapes from boar-breeding farms, populations of wild boars have solidly entrenched themselves in the Forest of Dean, Devon, and the Sussex-Kent area, and are spreading through the south.

Natural England, the government's advisory body on the environment, recognizes the boar as an indigenous animal, although it is concerned about controlling populations and thus provides boar-management guidance to the Department of Environment, Food, and Rural Affairs (DEFRA). Britain's national parks are pondering the reintroduction of eradicated species such as wolves, brown bears, lynx, beavers, and wild boars into the forests. Wildwood Discovery Park is a charity devoted to the reintroduction of these animals. Alladale Reserve in Scotland is running boar-sustainability studies with the aid of

Wild boars sorting through trash in England. (© Roxanne Blake/swns)

WildCRU at Oxford University. The debate is heating up: What animals do Britons really want roaming their island ark? Recently, DEFRA ruled that the wild boar is a threat to indigenous animals, and it's illegal to release a boar in Britain.

Animal lovers struggle to protect boars. For example, when the Hollywood actors Brad Pitt and Angelina Jolie leased a chateau in Miraval, near Aix-en-Provence, they discovered that boar hunting on their grounds verged on a sacred rite. In addition, the hunt was necessary to protect the vineyards against marauding boars; thus, the livelihoods of their neighbors were at issue. Jolie and Pitt battled to prevent the slaughter and the butchering of boars in their rather extensive backyard, but ultimately capitulated under pressure from their neighbors.

The divisions are clearest in Berlin, where boars are so numerous that they saunter down the boulevards, dig up playgrounds, and nurse their young on residents' doorsteps. To the chagrin of expert urban hunters, Berlin residents not only feed the boars, but they also interfere physically with control efforts. Reportedly, urban hunters have been jeered at, beaten, and otherwise threatened.

With a greater than threefold boar population increase in Germany, boars supersede their usual mischief of rooting up earth in cemeteries and gardens, terrorizing schools, and causing car wrecks, with 211 of them hit and killed in eight months in Berlin alone. They pose a potential health risk. Berlin scientists studying emerging diseases tested 141 boars killed by urban hunters and found that 18 percent tested positive for antibodies to leptospirosis, a disease that can be passed on to humans through the animal's urine.

In Paris, urban hunters trying to control boars face their own special problems. Boars have infiltrated suburban neighborhoods considered *quartiers sensibles,* such as in Val-Fourré in the commune of Mantes la-Jolie, west of Paris. These areas house a large population of unemployed immigrants, and violent gangs have engaged in recent rioting. Now boars have made their way into the world of tumbledown factories, slabs of concrete, and drug dealers. Urban hunters fear that when using firearms their bullets might ricochet off concrete and reignite violence, so they have resorted to bows and arrows, giving the boars a clear advantage. In one urban battue, fifty hunters managed to bag a single fox.

Around our village, bitter divisions between hunters and landowners have sprung up over boars damaging crops. Wanting to preserve game stocks, hunters offered to pay damages to farmers when grain prices were low and boar populations were moderate. Now, both have skyrocketed, and the hunters are still required to pay damages.

Roger Ramond alerted me to a midweek crisis meeting of the Fédération Départementale des Chasseurs du Loiret, and I went along with him. On arriving, we found two hundred acrimonious boar hunters had packed into the civic hall in the village of Saint-Brisson-sur-Loire. The local Federation president, Pascal Drouin, had the unenviable chore of delivering the painful economic figures and convincing the fuming hunters to vote on how to tax themselves. With the steep increase in crop destruction, the Federation's budget of €1.3 million for damages had a €140,000 shortfall. A majority of the damage came from five of the forty-one cantons, the culprit being corn-munching boars. Tax proposals were made: higher-priced bracelets for each boar bagged, increased licensing fees, varying lease taxes on specific properties depending on the level of damage.

The hunters wanted none of it. "We are controlling the populations, and we have to pay more to the farmers?" one shouted. They began accusing landowners, often hunters themselves, of profiteering. Despite the finger-pointing and rancor, the hunters would be forced to address the glaring deficit in their Federation's budget.

Considering that they invade the boulevards of many major European cities and wreak havoc on farms in the country, is it possible for a healthy boar to live a natural lifetime? The fact is that boars tend to die violently. Their preference for nocturnal activity is a direct adjustment to the diurnal habits of their sole predator, humans. Cities and towns sprawl to the edge of small forests and thus penetrate boar territory. A whole species that could function contentedly and successfully during the day has found the forest nightlife far more peaceful. Boars hunker down for the day in lairs in hidden parts of a forest, or in swampy thickets near ponds, or among inaccessible overgrowth along riverbanks.

In order to understand boar habits and the extent and nature of their movements, researchers have trapped hundreds of boars, fitted them with transmitter collars and tags, and monitored their ramblings on detailed maps. One fact they have learned is that boars are distinctly clean animals. The tracking transmissions show that even during the day a boar will leave the lair and find a spot at some distance to relieve himself. I observed this sage behavior among captive boars as well. In addition, while a mud bath may seem diametrically opposite to our notions of personal hygiene, boars relish rolling in mud because it assists with thermal regulation and the control of parasites, including ticks, fleas, and lice.

Once I watched a large male boar, slightly arthritic, rouse himself from his lair toward evening and then walk straight for a mud bath. The black slop glistened across his snout and all through his bristles and undercoat. He followed this up with a half hour of scratching against pine bark, stumps, and fallen trees. I was reminded of a middle-aged man getting up and performing prework ablutions. There is no mud that is muckier anywhere than that of La Puisaye. It is clay-filled and has the consistency of a black plaster slurry. The boar seemed delighted with it.

One of the difficulties boars experience is trying to groom parts of their bodies that are inaccessible due to their compact shape and inflexibility. To overcome this impediment, boars groom each other within the compagnie, using their teeth to chew parasites from the skin. This hygienic activity borders on the ritual, reinforcing the social fabric of the group. Mother sows groom piglets, and piglets groom each other. The elder boars seem to find it a soothing recreation in domestic lair-life.

Most of us who rarely encounter boars would find it difficult to believe that their odor could be pleasant, but one boar buff, Laurent Cabanau, gives quite the opposite impression. Writing in *Wild Boar in Europe,* he observes: "The smell of the wild boar is very heavy and pleasant, unlike a domestic pig. This smell reminds one of aniseed or bitumen after a storm, slightly peppery and musky. For us hunters and wild boar enthusiasts, its smell is a real perfume because when one has smelt it, clearly, they are not far away!"

When boars do sleep in the hidden shades of the forest, they tend to pile up on each other, particularly the young with their mothers or each other when their energy suddenly dips. Young boars, and even more mature rousses, clamor for spots between or against two or three larger females. Boars make depressions in the underbrush so that they resemble enormous birds in nests. Their snouts rest firmly on the earthen rim, their furry ears are erect, and their legs and tail are tucked under them. In anticipation of farrowing, giving birth, females prepare nests of grasses, leaves, and branches called farrowing chambers, a protective lair that can be three feet high.

When the sunlight angles from the west into the forest and the shadows deepen, a lead sow will stir, rustling in the leaves and lightly snapping twigs, snout in the evening air and ears pricked to capture any scents or sounds of danger. The boar snout is an almost supernatural instrument not only for scenting but also for its keen sense of touch, even during subterranean probing. The snout is surprisingly tender, and the hairs on the upper lip so sensitive that they detect the pulse of electric fences well in advance of being shocked.

At a signal from the lead sow, the compagnie will emerge, attentive to their leader's stream of communiqués: tail language, grunts, teeth chatter, fits and starts, and undoubtedly discreet odors that defy human sensory apparatus. Boars secrete scent for communicating identity, tracking, staking out territory, rut, and estrus. Sows cover their marcassins with their own scent at the earliest age, and the mother's identity is imprinted in their memories for nursing and socializing. The carpal glands behind the knees provide a constant trace for delineating territory and a trail back to the lair. A steroid pheromone is secreted by the boar's submaxillary salivary glands to induce estrus while the preputial gland at the tip of the boar's penis imbues the urine with a strong odor during rut. Interestingly, females indicate that they are in heat through a gland near their tear ducts. Boars possess wartlike chin glands as well as tusk glands for marking and communication.

Vendors of hunting paraphernalia tout their imitation boar secretion and urine products for luring hogs into traps and into range: Dominant Boar, Sow-N-Estrus, and Grim Reaper Wild Animal Attractant. Synthetic scents are used also to stimulate reproduction in captive boars and pigs.

Legends of boar migrations persist, but what researchers have learned from telemetry is that sounders stick to familiar territory unless weather conditions, lack of food, hunting, or competition forces them to search more viable domains. Most tagged or radio-monitored boars were found or recaptured within a three-mile area known as the "birth domain." Males may venture a good deal farther, up to 45 miles, but encounter peril if they do so since they range into unfamiliar territories and lack the security infrastructure of a group. Still, this wandering is essential for the health of the species, locating different sounders, different genetic pools. On a given night, a group of boars will cover from a mile and a half to eight miles, and over a year and a half cover an area up to twenty square miles, roughly the size of Manhattan Island.

The primary objective of boar forays is to search out the daily *repas*. A lead sow, having earned her position through age, experience, and cunning, leads the sounder, with the assistance of her lieutenant sows, to different feeding areas that change with the seasons. Boars create "deep furrows," rooting almost a foot under the ground for bulbs, tuberous roots, and rhizomes; or dig "shallow furrows" for grubs or worms as the ground warms. In autumn, the forest is usually abundant with acorns, chestnuts, and blackberries. Boars are opportunistic feeders. I've observed a boar spending nearly an hour removing individual woody scales and meticulously chewing them open for the tender inner seeds. I noticed another gnawing passionately on a deer's hoof. While they are reputed to eat almost anything from grass to cadavers, they select what pleases them most in times of abundance.

Boar life is generally peaceful but includes a lot of physical contact, including nose-to-nose greetings, nudging, grooming, and boar-piling in the lair. A certain amount of squabbling is involved along with scolding and jockeying for dominance, which sends bristles erect and ears cocked, and is accompanied by grunts, squealing, grinding of teeth, and threatening charges. However, real boar fights do develop over territory or mating rights. Competing males will approach each other stiff-leggedly posturing with erect bristles. Often serious boar disputes are settled quickly with a demonstration of overwhelming strength, one boar aggressively leveraging another, shoulder to shoulder or through aggressive frontal engagement. But these engagements are largely ritualistic.

More violent contests arise when the males are more evenly matched in physical prowess and determination. Their battles can be dramatic, given the power and ferocity of boars when truly challenged. As so often described in mythic confrontations, boars actually do foam at the mouth in rage, and the battle escalates from jostling and butting into violent lateral clashes in which tusks can be employed against the adversary in slashing and upward-gouging motions. They are at each other's necks, ears, and front legs, biting and slashing. The episode is usually accompanied by loud grunts and squealing.

Fortunately, boars are well protected for these engagements by a shield of thick skin and fur around their chests and necks. During rut, hormones trigger the development of a layer of thick protective fat in these same areas. Fighting can result in the death of one or both boars, but this is extremely rare. Usually, one boar must concede and retreat to heal his wounds.

As with much of the animal world, boar mating follows a ritual. The battle-tested, and often fatigued, male has earned the right to seek out a receptive female manifesting the physical and behavioral effects of estrus, which in boars lasts only twenty-four to thirty-six hours. The courtship includes nuzzling, biting, licking, and scent marking, all aimed at stimulating the senses. The male mounts the sow and enters a corkscrew-shaped penis for up to twenty minutes. Then the whole ritual begins again with another sow in heat.

One of the prime reasons boar populations explode is that sows can be fertile most of the year. Sexual maturity can start at eight months. Thus, a female born in spring reaches puberty by December. In certain years, rut comes early, so it is possible for a sow to have two litters during that twelve-month cycle. Each sow can bear young for up to eight years.

When the piglets are born, they chew through their own umbilical cords and begin nursing immediately. Their brown and tan stripes offer perfect camouflage in the farrowing chamber lined with straw and leaves of the same colors. The powerful senses of the newborns become acute within hours, and those senses lead them to an awareness of territory and social order within days, including establishing which nursing teat belongs to whom.

After the first few days, the young will venture out of the chamber. Within ten days, the lead sow will visit the new families and begin reassembling the sounder, with its new members mixing and rollicking with each other. When it's time for feeding, a mother sow will give short, loud grunts and the young will split up, knowing which mother

Marcassins (boar piglets) sleeping. (© Martin Ruegner/Getty Images)

is theirs by sound and scent. Within three weeks, the piglets begin eating vegetation, though weaning may take four months. The compagnie offers such a tight social system that if a mother sow is killed, the other females tend the orphans.

As the piglets grow, their games and curiosities begin to prepare them for life in the sounder or in the mating ritual. What is playful combat, shoulder butting, and minor squabbling will transform into a means for determining rank. Within four months, the lovely stripes fade into a more uniform brownish red coat and the rousses learn their own rankings behind the others, although the rousses that are offspring of high-ranking sows enjoy some feeding and social privileges denied others of their age group.

At between nine and eighteen months, the young males lose their social privileges and are shunned from the group. At first, they form small groups of their own and stay within proximity of the sounder. But as puberty sets in, they begin to compete with each other, becoming further isolated, and with the exception of mating they remain solitary for the rest of their lives.

For many hunters, confronting a massive male boar with trophy tusks offers the ultimate thrill, a moment of personal legend. For me, it's always seeing the compagnie in action at dusk on a path beside the canal or at the edge of a field that creates a sense of awe. However, the mere fact that I could see boars on a regular basis was further evidence of the overpopulation problem.

As I've become older, sleep is more fitful, even impossible at times. I lie awake thinking, Why not go out to the woods? It's no mystery where the boars live — Breteau, Champoulet, and the lakes around Bléneau. One night, I woke at 3 a.m., the moonlight pouring into our bedroom. The lights on the place de l'Église and the church next to our house had long been out, but the car under the chestnut tree was fully illuminated. All sounds were magnified — the car door, the ignition, and wheels — against the silent walls of the upper village. I drove through the middle of our blacked-out village and onto the narrow wooded roads to the rue des Postillons, where we'd seen boars before, as far as Dammarie-en-Puisaye. A number of deer appeared and hares like small deer themselves near cornfields and meadows.

Finally I did spot a boar trundling off the road and disappearing into the understory of a copse. I was near the Étang du Château at nearly 4 a.m. This lake, mainly hidden from the road, is almost completely surrounded by woods. Only a small chateau with a dam appears at one end. Thicket comes down to the water, offering perfect boar cover, and I stayed for an hour, the full moon illuminating the entire landscape, the woods full of sounds: owls, the mutterings of ducks, the twigs snapping under the hoofs of deer or boars. Night after night, I would drive to the chateau's lake and encounter no one, only the sounds of animals. The boars I'd see would appear all too briefly to be considered observation. But I understood the comfort of this hour, the only peace to be found.

_____

Chapter Nine

Myths and Monsters

U NLIKE OTHER students who also elected to take Latin, I didn't mind translating *De Bello Gallico,* Julius Caesar's commentaries on the Gallic Wars. It wasn't the warfare that attracted me so much as the lucidity of the writing; the people and places in history rose out of the original language of the ancients. The experience was entirely new. My Latin teachers, gentlemanly and somewhat otherworldly in a large urban school, must have explained that history, particularly where war was concerned, was often a self-serving invention of the victor. Still, everything I knew as a child about the Gauls came from Julius Caesar, and if I could have telescoped through time, I would have been shocked to see myself living in the same region as Alésia, site of Caesar's great victory over Vercingetorix.

It wasn't long ago that French children were taught that their national history began with "nos ancêtres les Gaulois." It didn't matter whether their family background was North African or Vietnamese. They all learned of their ancestors, les Gaulois, and the warrior Vercingetorix, who waged an inspired rebellion against the Romans. He managed to unify tribes and make a stand at Alésia near Dijon, but the Gallic warriors lost in a siege masterfully orchestrated by Julius Caesar, despite the fact that the Roman legions were vastly outnumbered. While the Gauls suffered a decisive defeat, France was recompensed with its first hero in Vercingetorix, a symbol of Gallic valor and courage. Honoring the embodiment of these virtues, Napoleon III erected a memorial statue of Vercingetorix at Alésia, a twenty-three-foot head-to-toe marvel of historical inaccuracy.

In 1959, two famous cartoon characters appeared: Asterix, an intrepid Gallic warrior, and his enormous sidekick Obelix, inventions of the writer René Goscinny and the illustrator Albert Uderzo. Obelix possessed a voracious appetite, and his favorite food was wild boar, which he hunted with Asterix. Both characters are often shown carting off a boar for a feast. Obelix, sometimes hefting a boar under each arm, was known to eat six boars at a sitting. Asterix's and Obelix's infatuation with boar meat had a well-known historical basis, for boar provided an important food source. However, the boar's significance for the Gauls and in antiquity was far greater than that.

One of the most important Celtic works of art, a near-life-sized bronze boar sculpture, was found among a cache of Celtic artifacts in Neuvy-en-Sullias, just twenty miles south of my home. The boar assumes an aggressive stance with highly stylized bristles erect, and its snout is thrust forward, lip raised. Its compact body radiates power and confrontation. This image of the boar appears repeatedly in Celtic artifacts found in disparate parts of western Europe. One such brass boar, an insignia of the Gauls, was found on a beach at Soulac-sur-Mer and reproduced for jewelry. Its picture also was used on a recent €1.30 stamp.

The Celts practiced animism and were led spiritually by druids, who performed an array of offices that included settling disputes, transmitting oral tradition, and presiding over religious ceremonies. The Celts believed spirits manifested themselves in animal and human forms or were imbued in trees, rivers, rocks, springs, and mountains. The wild boar was among their sacred animals.

The Gauls, too, revered the wild boar for its fearsome defense. Boar iconography ornamented their war standards, horns, helmets, and shields the way the Romans displayed the *aquila,* the imperial eagle (although Romans used boar imagery as well). While some Gallic tribes wielded boar heads constructed out of sheet bronze on the battlefield, along with war-trophy human heads, to terrify enemies, animal iconography was omnipresent in their art, appearing in carved reliefs, architecture, statues, jewelry, and coinage. Horses, bulls, and boars, animals that may have held religious significance, were favored subjects.

Gallic coins are often highly abstract. Coin dealers today sometimes refer to them as "Piccassoesque" or "cubist." Boars appeared on gold and silver staters, drachmas, and bronze potins. Gallic tribes began casting and striking coins modeled after the Greek gold staters that they received through trade, or in payment for their services as mercenaries. Roman coins also provided the Gauls with iconographic models.

While Greek and Roman coins were decorated with sober, dignified images of wreathed heads and realistically rendered horses, the Gallic coins were wildly stylized and disjointed, only vaguely reminiscent of their refined model coins. I struggled to identify outrageous-looking or small, hidden boars amid symbols, circles, and loops.

I found the coins so stunning that I browsed numismatic catalogs for Celtic boar potins on the off chance I could purchase one at a reasonable price. This quest led me, like any modern person, to eBay. I typed "boar" into "All Categories" and discovered a myriad of boar objects awaiting bids: Black Forest boar trophies; boar silverware; traditional formal boar-hunting buttons; boar-tusk carvings; boar pendants, necklaces, and bracelets; boar engravings, paintings, and statues; and boar stamps from Borneo, Russia, and Afghanistan. Among these items was a second-century AD terra-cotta Roman oil lamp with a wild-boar relief on the discus cover: a museum in Wales was auctioning off some of its stored acquisitions to raise revenue.

The initial trap of eBay, at least in my case, was assuming that I could never make the winning bid. I bid £35, and to my surprise, the oil lamp, admittedly not in perfect condition, arrived in Paris along with the museum director's certificate of authenticity. The reservoir cover was thin, partly blackened, and chipped at the edges, but the image of a dashing boar was skillfully rendered. The object, nearly two thousand years old, somehow transcended any sensation of ownership. It sat on my desk, a finely crafted alien from another age.

eBay was decidedly dangerous. How amazing to be "winning" a small museum of antiquities! A growing population of boar statuettes from Japan, China, Java, Italy, and England competed for desk space with the Roman lamp. Religious engravings, collector's postcards, and a 75-pfennig note depicting a saint and a boar hung on my wall.

Then I purchased three Gallic coins. The first was bronze, smaller than a Levi's fly button, and rated as rare and in very good condition. The Ambiani tribe, once to be found in the area of modern-day Amiens and a part of the larger Gallia Belgica, had minted it around 50 BC, concurrent with Caesar's military exploits in Gaul. The boar was clearly based on highly stylized boar renderings on Greek pottery, in which the bristles down the spine are so exaggerated that they looked like a marlin's fin. In the Gallic version, the bristles were almost absurdly disproportional, appearing like a loom or a harp across the boar's back.

The second coin, much less elaborate but almost twice the size of the first, was a *potin à la tête d'indien,* with an even more abstract version of a boar. The obverse side featured a head wearing a laureate that resembled a band and feathers, thus the name. This crude-bronze alloy coin was minted by the Leuci tribe that lived in northern Burgundy and the Champagne region.

My favorite coin, however, was an extrafine 150 BC Celtiberian bronze from Castulo, Hispania. The boar was magnificent: ears erect, long snout with distinct tusks, a bulging eye, proportionate bristles, and tail that looped with attentiveness. It had a joyfully childish quality. Even the large-nosed laureate head on the obverse side appeared to be mocking the Greeks.

My bank voided my credit card for erratic purchasing activity, tossing a bucket of ice water on an impassioned bid for a nineteenth-century Japanese painting of a boar in moonlight. That jolted me to my senses, and the eBay phase of my life ended after three frenzied weeks. Fortunately, the financial damage was minor. But these items occupying my desk raised a question: What did the boar emblem mean to the ancients?

The Romans associated the Gauls with boars. On Trajan's Column, a boar is a Gallic emblem in the depiction of Trajan's triumphs in Rome's northern provinces. Gallic warriors invoked the boar spirit to lead them aggressively into battle and inspire cunning maneuvers on defense. A boar's hide was thought to impart healing powers to the wounded. Outside of the martial sphere, the boar was a symbol of wealth, fertility, and creativity, associated with the sun, light, and the New Year. While in Norse myth the golden-bristled boar served Frey as a luminous steed, the Roman-Gallo version is represented in a floor mosaic from Saint-Roman-en-Gal: a woman bundled in heavy blue cloth riding a boar personifying winter. Arduinna, the Celtic version of Diana and namesake for a boar-teeming region, the Ardennes, was rendered riding a boar sidesaddle in a skimpy tunic, sword raised. The wild boar remains such a potent symbol of the Ardennes that at one Ardennes highway service plaza a three-story-high wild-boar statue called *Woinic* has been erected. I drove to the plaza just to see the world's largest boar, 55 tons of welded steel, slowly rotate in the rain.

As the Roman oil lamp on my desk demonstrated, Romans shared the Gallic enthusiasm for the boar emblem. The boar served as an insignia for Octavian's Twentieth Legion campaigns in what is now Spain, Germany, and Britain, as well as for his Tenth Legion during the Balkans campaign. Nero's First Legion, in its defense of the Danube, also fought under the boar insignia.

But, in general, the boar didn't carry the same symbolic and practical weight for the Romans that it did for Celtic and Germanic tribes. While the Romans, like the Greeks and Celts, used domestic animals in religious sacrifices, boars played their part in bloody arena spectacles where different species fights were staged among elephants, rhinos, buffaloes, tigers, leopards, and wolves. Some boars were trained via feeding time for more passive entertainment. At feasts, one might arrive at the side of a servant dressed up as Orpheus, amusing the guests of wealthy aristocrats with this testimonial to Orpheus's famous gift for taming animals.

In Roman art, boars were rendered most often in hunting scenes or illustrations of Greek myths assimilated into Roman theology. Boars are widely found in floor mosaics such as that in the colorful House of the Wild Boar in Pompeii; in Vittoria and Armerina Piazzas in Sicily; in the dining room of a home in El Jem, southern Tunisia. While the wild boars appear on Roman sarcophagi, coins, chariots, reliefs, and vessels, they also became a centerpiece of epicurean pleasures, if not outright

Woinic, world's largest boar, being transported to the gateway of the Ardennes. (© François Nascimbeni/AFP)

gluttony, at banquets. The Romans created hunting parks or *vivariums* for the boar and other wild animals, ensuring that boar meat was always readily available. Pliny the Elder reported in *Natural History* that serving whole boars at banquets became so popular in high society that it sparked criticism of Roman manners: "now-a-days two or three boars are consumed, not at one entertainment, but as forming the first course only." Obelix, if not outdone, had rivals in gluttonous imperial Rome.

The surreal banquet for Nero depicted in Petronius's *Satyricon* provides the ultimate vision of this gluttony. Guests were already stuffed when an enormous wild boar was served wearing a Phrygian liberty cap. Its tusks were adorned with woven palm-leaf baskets full of Syrian and Theban dates. Piglets sculpted of mincemeat-filled pastries signified that the boar was a "brood-sow." A servant cut into a boar filled with live birds:

> Drawing his hunting knife, he made a furious lunge and gashed open the boar's flank, from which there flew out a number of fieldfares. Fowlers stood ready with their rods and immediately caught the birds as they fluttered about the table. Then Trimalchio directed each guest to be given his bird, and this done, added, "Look what elegant acorns this wildwood pig fed on."

While Petronius's verse-prose work is a caricature of Nero's era, scholars have regarded it a valuable window on Roman life.

Because Roman art and literature assimilated the Greek myths, the Romans were versed in the stories of the gods, half-gods, and mortals; a few of the most famous involved boars. Ovid's epic work *Metamorphoses*, in part a compilation of Greek stories meant to transcend the ages, includes a rendition of "Meleäger and the Calydonian Boar." During harvest, King Oéneus egregiously failed to pay tribute to Diana, leading the goddess to unleash a fantastical boar to take vengeance:

> Blood and fire were aglow in his eyes; his neck
>   was stiff
> with bristles as firm as serried spears or the
>   stakes on a rampart
> His massive flanks were flecked with a spray of
>   seething foam
> from his grunting snorts; his tusks were as
>   long as an Indian elephant's.
> Lightning flashed from his mouth and his
>   breath-blasts shriveled the grassland.

The destructive Calydonian Boar was a place-bound Chthonic monster, requiring a constellation of Olympian heroes to subdue it. Some paid a dear price, suffering torn tendons, burst bowels, and other grave injuries. In the end, the huntress Atalanta's arrow slowed the boar, and Meleäger drove his lance through its heart. Meleäger then angered the hunting party when he awarded the boar's skin and head with the great white tusks to Atalanta, igniting jealousies that would lead to his own demise.

Some classists find Ovid's descriptions of the Calydonian Boar too "ridiculous" and prefer the more sober Greek rendition that came from the oral tradition and first appeared in book 11 of the *Iliad*. In the Homeric version "heard in song," jealousies over the head and skin of the Calydonian Boar provoked a war between Curetes and the Aetolians.

The Calydonian Boar has been rendered on Grecian vases, Roman reliefs, and Renaissance marbles, but isn't alone among Greek place-bound boar monsters. The other was the Erymanthian Boar of Mount Erymanthos, unleashed this time by Artemis, Diana's Greek counterpart, to ravage farmlands. Hercules, strongest of the Greek heroes, was assigned to capture it alive as the fourth of his famous twelve penitential labors.

Hercules' task was so laden with difficulties, primarily the boar's ability to run circles around the mountain, that he was compelled to seek advice from the underworld centaur Chiron, who advised chasing the boar in deep snow to slow it. Versions of the capture vary, but ultimately the boar became either entrapped in a snow-filled ravine or entangled with Hercules in a huge snowball.

In most of the artwork, Hercules is scantily dressed despite the snow. He hefts the enormous boar over his shoulder, alive, of course, and diligently delivers it to a mortified King Eurystheus, who assigned the twelve labors. In one brilliant vase painting, Hercules is shown preparing to drop the beast into a storage pot where cowering Eurystheus had taken refuge.

Meleäger and Hercules get the best of their supernatural boars. Even Theseus, Hercules' heroic comrade and eventual king of Athens, had among his duties the chore of dispatching with the troublesome boar of Krommyon, a sow in fact. Ulysses in his youth had a tougher time dispatching the ferocious Mount Parnassus Boar. The boar, with raised bristles and "fire flashing from his eyes," ripped a gash above Ulysses' knee, but the hero managed to drive his spear through the boar's right shoulder before passing out. The scar would later reveal Ulysses' identity when he returned, disguised as a beggar, to his home in Ithaca.

One supernatural boar does triumph over a famous hero, the beautiful Adonis, Venus's mortal lover. This ancient myth comes to us in its most popular version through Ovid's Orpheus recitals.

Adonis, born of his own sister and grandfather, grew into a beautiful man. Cupid unwittingly nicked the breast of his own mother, Venus, with an arrow, and the goddess of love became obsessed with Adonis, abandoning her haunts in heaven to cling to him or shadow his movements. She begged Adonis from the beginning to avoid in the hunt aggressive creatures that bare their teeth, but dogs had aroused a boar from its lair, and after Adonis speared it to no effect, the boar "buried its tusks deep in his groin." Venus was left to discover Adonis in pooled blood. In bitter grief, she proclaimed a memorial, the annual reenactment through blooming red anemones.

The Venus and Adonis story has been one of the richest subjects for artists and writers since classical times. Titian and then Shakespeare focused on the frustration of Venus as Adonis disregards her seduction in order to participate in the hunt.

> 'Tis true, 'tis true; thus was Adonis slain:
> He ran upon the boar with his sharp spear,
> Who did not whet his teeth at him again,
> But by a kiss thought to persuade him there;
> And nuzzling in his flank, the loving swine
> Sheathed unaware the tusk in his soft groin.
>
> "Had I been tooth'd like him, I must confess,
> With kissing him I should have kill'd him first."
> (lines 1111–18)

Death of Adonis (1709), by Giuseppe-Mazzuoli. (Yair Haklai)

Shakespeare's *Venus and Adonis,* an erotically taunting mini-epic, was his most popular published work in his own time.

The romantic Irish legend of Grainne and Diarmuid has striking parallels with the Venus and Adonis myth. In the Celtic tale, Grainne was betrothed to be the second wife of the aging chieftain Fionn Mac Cumhaill, but at the celebratory feast she encountered and fell in love with one of Fionn's best warriors, Diarmuid. When loyal Diarmuid resisted Grainne's sexual overtures, Grainne, taking no chances, cast a love spell on him. With Diarmuid hopelessly in her powers, the couple fled across Ireland and hid in the wilds with furious Fionn ceaselessly pursuing them.

After years spent as fugitives and Grainne becoming pregnant, destiny caught up to them in the form of the wild boar of Benn Gulban heath. Diarmuid's dogs roused him in a dream to hunt the boar, even though Grainne futilely tried to prevent him from leaving. On the heath, Diarmuid encountered Fionn, who reminded Diarmuid of his bond of *geasa* (a curselike taboo) against the hunt. The Ben Gulban boar is, in fact, Diarmuid's murdered younger half-brother, resurrected and transformed by the touch of a druid's wand. Warned in youth never to hunt boar, Diarmuid found his fate sealed by Fionn's devices. He accused Fionn: "to slay me that thou hast made this hunt, O Fionn; and if it be here I am fated to die I have no power now to shun it."

Diarmuid ended up with his bowels and entrails wrapped at his ankles, yet still he managed to drive his broken sword into the boar's brain. The half-brothers, boar and hero, vanquished each other, though Fionn might have saved Diarmuid with the magic healing waters he allowed to slip through his fingers.

All the boar objects and images on or around my desk allude to myths, religions, and ancient cultures, including one beautiful golden boar that came from China. A fourteen-year-old, Alexander, was visiting with Mary's extended family and fell in love with the Celtic coins I showed him, asking if I could help him buy a *potin à la tête d'indien* with fifty euros he'd saved. I had never been a collector of objects until my eBay frenzy, and I realized that my zeal had left me. I found a box and some bubble wrap for the coins and Roman lamp and asked Alexander's mother if she could give them to him at Christmas. Still, I did keep the Picassoesque 150 BC Iberian boar and the starburst. Like the ancients, I am captivated by the vision of boars and celestial illumination.

Chapter Ten

Travels

Tuscany, Tyrrhenian Islands, and Boars

MARY HAD ASSUMED that my enthusiasm for boars would be short-lived like my ephemeral interest in fly fishing after a couple of fruitless hours on a fished-out French river or mushrooming after learning of the accidental poisoning of a neighbor's family. To her mind, I had observed enough boars to suit even the most avid boar buff. In addition, I had littered my desk with boar icons, some admittedly trashy, and tested the polite attention of our friends with boar prattle. Now, after scheming in front of my replica of *Porcellino*, Pietro Tacca's boar masterpiece that resides in Florence, I posed an idea to Mary: "What do you think about traveling to Tuscany this summer and then spending a couple of days in Corsica before going on to Sardinia?"

We often vacationed in Sardinia in the cheaper off-season, taking the convenient overnight ferry from Marseille. This vacation is invariably a financial strain, and the trip I was proposing at high season was outright extravagant, but my suggestion was not summarily dismissed. "On what?" she asked bluntly.

While I extolled Tacca's sculpture, the Mediterranean region's fame for boar-hunting tradition, and classic *cinghiale* cuisine, Mary looked like a kidnap victim. It obviously wasn't a matter of going to such coveted vacation destinations; it was that a precious vacation would be devoted to "more boars." Mary wasn't won over exactly, but she threw up her hands. "You make the arrangements then."

And so I did. We'd drive from Paris through the Swiss Alps to Livorno, catching the ferry to Bastia on Corsica, and then after exploring the length of the island, finally crossing the Golfo dell'Asinara to Sardinia. One consolation for Mary was that Corsica Ferries, which runs between Livorno and Sardinia, is the only line that allows dogs on the decks and in the cabin, and she wanted to bring our dog, Jake, with us if I was going to be off pursuing boars.

Looking for a convenient town and lodgings where we could pass a couple of days in Tuscany and then comfortably make our way to the port, we chanced upon the Albergo Roma in Casciana Terme, a town with charm but little touristic interest, situated in the gentle Pisan hills. The Roma, a stately manor converted into a hotel, offered spacious high-ceilinged rooms and accepted dogs with unusual enthusiasm from both the establishment and the guests congregating in the lounge or sipping drinks and playing cards around the swimming pool. The many elderly clients had come to soothe their miseries in the extensive thermal baths, which were originally known to the Romans and have provided cures for over two millennia.

Jake, a Cavalier King Charles spaniel who spends most of his time in Paris, was accustomed to strangers, even ailing ones, lavishing attention on him, but he focused on a gritty barking exchange with a grand griffon vendéen interned behind a chain-link fence.

That evening at the charming Ristorante Il Merlo, we enjoyed the *cinghiale antipasta,* a selection of thinly sliced boar sausages and prosciutto, followed by *pettole con basilico e pistacchi.* We allowed ourselves an extra two days to tour western Tuscany. In Volterra, cinghiale could be found on almost every restaurant menu, including boar stew *alla moda di Volterra.* The Palazzo dei Pretorio has the "Porcellino Tower," featuring a rotund wild boar carved in stone and suspended on a ledge over the tourist-packed piazza.

Back at the Albergo Roma, Jake and the scruffy grand griffon resumed their barking rivalry, and ailing old folks fussed over our spoiled dog in the reception lounge. I asked the Canadian desk clerk if boar hunting was common in the area.

"It isn't hunting season, but I can arrange a hunt for you in October."

"No, I was just curious."

"Well, the purest boars in Italy are found in Maremma, just south of here where the legendary Italian cowboys come from. That's our version of the 'Wild West,'" he smiled. "Buffalo Bill Cody brought his show over here once and challenged the Italians to a rodeo. The Maremma cowboys trounced him. The country is rugged, and the biggest boars in Italy are found there. That dog out back is a prizewinner. The Italian boar-hunting champion. He hunts with the owner in Maremma. Of course, we have boars right here in Casciana Terme too. They just march into town when they feel like it."

Jake had been quarrelling with the Italian boar-hunting champion! The clerk said, "If you are really interested in boars, I'll show you something."

He went to the key rack and signaled for us to follow him. He took us out past the pool, with a view of the church belltower and soaring evening swallows that at dusk will give way to bats. The Italian boar-hunting champion eagerly greeted us with loud barking and front paws pressed against the fence. Our guide led us to the white doors of a garage, which he opened, revealing a gray Alfa Romeo sedan packed in with hunting-dog crates and a makeshift shrine to boars, dogs, and hunters: two boar's-head trophies presided on either side of a large black-and-white photograph of the prized griffon. A trophy cup acted like a convex mirror, reflecting a warp version of the garage.

"There you are, the champion," he announced.

"How many Italian boar-hunting champions are there?"

"That's him."

All around the small garage, crammed with the usual tires and boxes, were the typical boar-hunting photograph poses: wild-boar carcasses meticulously arranged in rows with the largest boars in the middle; dogs embraced by a few kneeling men or held on leads while large groups of men pose behind the carnage. Some photographs seemed to portray the entire population of a village's men. Not one woman or child was evident. Boar hunting tends to be a gender-specific activity (although there are exceptions even in France and the United States, given the women's hunting associations), but judging from the photographs, Italian boar hunting is an exclusively masculine activity.

I'd learn later that boar hunting is even more regulated in Italy than France. Rules call for shorter hunting seasons, restricted hunting locations, and mandatory group organization in the interest of safety. Local boar societies operate under a code. The social anthropologist Joan Weibel-Orlando returned to the village of her family's Tuscan origins and analyzed the exclusively male Società del Cinghiale. Its members not only possessed mastery of their weapons and dogs but also had to be "true men": "A hunt squad member must demonstrate certain positive and manly personality traits — reliability, physical strength, bravery, cool headedness, trustworthiness, and group loyalty. To be a good *cinghialai* is to be *un buon'uomo.*" The typical Società del Cinghiale has its own meetinghouse, equipped with game refrigerators and hooks for butchering. Women are not forbidden, but they are hardly encouraged into the world of male bonding that can include heavy drinking, vulgar jokes, and the detailed recounting of a glorious kill.

After our garage tour was over, we decided to take a late stroll. Italian towns in the evening, even ones that attract a large population suffering rheumatic ailments, have a festive atmosphere: children and dogs liberated from the heat and old folks segregated into male and female symposia. The *gelaterie* blaze with bright lights above mirrors, stainless steel, and an array of colorful ice creams. Still, I couldn't help imagining Tuscan boars mobilizing for night forays at the fringes of town. The Italian boar-hunting champion was undoubtedly taunted by hints of their odors.

The next day, in heat already brutal by late morning, we drove to Lucca and imprudently entered the interior maze of the walled city. Our search for an exit led us to the Saint Michele in Foro, an eccentric Pisan Romanesque church, Saint Michele at the crest of the façade with metal wings that could flap at festivals or be retracted in high winds. The oversized front façade featured loggia with arcades of pink and white, elaborately carved marble pillars, each one unique, and unusual secular statues and marble marquetry depicting animals in profile, including several black wild boars.

We forged ahead in the fatiguing weather to pay homage to Tacca's *Porcellino* in Florence. Mary protested ardently at first but relented on seeing Sunday traffic streaming in the opposite direction toward the beaches. However, the July crowds swarmed the piazzas. At the arcade of the Mercato Nuovo, foreigners had lined up to pose next to *Porcellino,* adorning him with staw hats, baseball caps, two-fingered devil's horns, and scarves. Teenage girls kissed him, evoking images of *Beauty and the Beast.* Under the brightly gleaming bronze snout, coins clinked through the fountain grate. All this took place against a backdrop of stacked leather purses, scarves, and reproductions of Michelangelo's *David.*

This was hardly my first pilgrimage to pay homage to *Porcellino.* In 1973, I had taken a job packing and shipping dresses in a small-town garment factory to earn my first plane ticket to Europe. I knew nothing about paintings, sculptures, or the like, but my travels led me to Pietro Tacca's magnificent bronze boar, its snout worn to a polished gleam. The High Renaissance sculpture was affectionately nicknamed *Porcellino,* or piglet.

Each year students and tourists stream by the thousands to give *Porcellino* a pat. I was no different, deranging a few of the sculpture's molecules, a common form of erosion caused by human adoration, the sort of damage more often reserved for the feet, hands, or bosoms of saints. Even though in *Porcellino*'s case the subject is secular, the statue still possesses modest supernatural powers: if you rub the snout, you will return soon to Florence.

The second time I visited *Porcellino* was in 1986, and it was momentous. I had just met Mary, a slim woman with long, mousy blond hair and bright blue eyes, on the train to Florence. At this time, she was living in Paris with two cats and a cello. We ended up married, leading to my unforeseen life in France.

I've returned more than a half-dozen times to the sculpture and can't

Porcellino, by Pietro Tacca, Mercato Nuovo, Florence. (Radomił Binek)

scoff at the "lucky" piglet's powers. On each visit, I'm reminded how strikingly visual wild boars are, which accounts in part for the popularity of Tacca's bronze, one of the most famous pieces of animal art. The boar more than makes up for what it lacks in beauty and grace with a nobility of spirit, a stirring sense of power and awareness, the male sporting curled, bladelike tusks captured in stunning detail.

If Pietro Tacca, court sculptor of the Grand Dukes of Tuscany, could be transported four centuries into the future, he would hardly be surprised that his equestrian bronzes have remained celebrated monuments, and he might be pleased that his *Four Moors* are now esteemed masterpieces at the port in Livorno. Tacca took over Giambologna's celebrated Florentine workshop and foundry; and yet like most artists never felt he was justly rewarded for his painstaking oversight of all stages in a monument's making, including the hellish casting in damp winter that compromised his health. Still, there is no way that he could have anticipated that *Porcellino,* his meticulous bronze casting of a boar rising alert on his haunch, would enlist tourists' good-luck pilgrimages and become one of the symbols of Florence.

Like many other admirers, I assumed that the statue at the Mercato Nuovo was the original. Not so. As the first *Porcellino* bestowed good luck, the public inadvertently began to destroy it, thousands of hands and kisses wearing the detail down to a smooth bright luster. In 1962, multiple replicas were made in the Ferdinando Marinelli Artistic Foundry, and the original Tacca boar was placed in protective custody at the Bargello Museum, where it is now on display. No official would want to undermine the tourist-attracting value of the boar, so a replica has served as a stand-in, the public, for the most part, oblivious to the switch.

However, the matter of replicas is complicated. Tacca's original *Porcellino* isn't an original at all but a reproduction cast in 1620 from a marble boar of the Hellenistic period revered by baroque sculptors. The marble boar, *Il Cinghiale*, residing in the ducal collection at the Uffizi, is itself a replica of a Greek sculpture that has been lost or destroyed. The original was believed to be part of a larger hunting group forming a fountain.

Porcellino is also a fountain of sorts. The long, distinct snout of Tacca's boar provides an irresistible slope for rolling coins so that they drop from the erect ears, between furrowed brows, past the fearsome tusks, and off the tip into the fountain water, represented as a pond surrounded by frogs, snakes, and plant life. More often coins are placed in the mouth where they stream back out, followed by a wish and a pat on the nose. But most often, the public more economically rubs *Porcellino*'s snout to earn good luck. Young children sometimes burst into tears at the mere suggestion of touching such a weird creature, even in statue form. To underline the profound effect *Porcellino* might have on a child's psyche, a plaque reminds us of the Hans Christian Andersen fairy tale in which a boy dreams of flying through the Uffizi Gallery on the back of a bronze boar.

After garnering good luck from *Porcellino,* visitors can stroll a few blocks to enjoy dining at the highly regarded restaurant the Osteria del Cinghiale Blanco. The restaurant features classic Italian boar dishes:

The Bronze Pig (1928), illustration by F. J. Sherman from
Hans Christian Andersen's *Fairy Tales.*

antipasto di cinghiale, pappardelle al cinghiale, and *cinghiale alla marem-
mana con polenta.*

When Mary and I first met, we were not unlike most travelers who
experienced their first boar *civet, pasta con cinghiale,* or *cinghiale prosciutto* in Tuscany. We tried the Italian classic *pici con ragù di cinghiale,*
a boar stew simmered in red wine with olive oil, tomatoes, onions, garlic, juniper berries, and rosemary and served on thick pasta. Variations
are found among the *primo platti* of most authentic Tuscan restaurants.
Another classic is boar with porcini mushrooms and black olives, all
fruits of autumn. We tasted the robust flavors of *ragù di cinghiale* for the
first time under the strings of twinkling lights of La Torre di Gargonza

terrace, with bats looping wildly between the pines and along the Castello walls.

Mary is a big fan of *Porcellino,* and she even waited patiently with Jake while I rushed through the Bargello Museum. But in the end, Mary and Jake withered in the city crowds and heat. Mary was anxious to return to Casciana Terme in the hills, to the cool stately rooms of the Albergo Roma and the comfort of its pool surrounded by amiably inebriated guests mulling over their cards.

With our stay in Tuscany over, we acquired picnic supplies for the ferry trip and photographed Tacca's *Four Moors,* slaves torturously bound to a column surmounted by Bradinelli's Ferdinand I. Standing on the rear deck of the *Corsica Serena* and watching Livorno shrink in the drift of diesel fumes, I returned to boar musings. Conjecture persists that cinghiali arrived in Corsica by the Tyrrhenian Sea from the Italian mainland. Boars are exceptional swimmers, but that particular swim would represent an extraordinary feat even for the most intrepid boar. Interestingly, these waters are a part of a triangular protected marine reserve for the boar's remote relative, the cetaceans, and we had the joy of seeing fin whales and dolphins along the flanks of ferries on previous trips.

As Livorno faded, Elba appeared ever larger, an island definitely within boar swimming range from the Maremma coastline. But could a boar swim the thirty-plus miles from Elba to Corsica? Maybe a top-notch athlete could. The distance between Bonifacio at the southern tip of Corsica and Santa Teresa Gallura in northern Sardinia is only six miles, making a boar crossing conceivable. Two million years ago during the Pleistocene, *Sus* species inhabited the islands but became extinct. They later returned to the pigless islands during the early Neolithic period.

Word was out that the Corsica Ferries from Livorno were dog-friendly. Queuing up to recover our car, we encountered an array of breeds and temperaments on the deck, making the ferry a veritable Noah's Ark of dogs. We disembarked at Bastia and stayed at a bed and breakfast in an almost inaccessible mountain village on the rugged cape. I had reserved a table at Le Pirate, a starred restaurant situated at the water's edge, after reading that among their specialties was *la côte de cochon noir de Bigorre*. I had naively thought that *cochon noir* had something to do with boar when in fact *cochon noir de Bigorre* was a black-hog breed associated with Gascony. We were obliged to make a long descent through a myriad of hairpin turns for highly touted pork chops.

We decided over dinner that we'd wait for our arrival in Sardinia to enjoy the ocean and concentrate on exploring the interior of Corsica. Designated the Parc Naturel Régional de Corse, it represents 40 percent of the island's land area. It has been said that the park was created to prevent Corsicans from developing the island for economic self-sufficiency after episodes of secessionist violence in the 1970s.

Throughout Mediterranean history, imperialistic cultures — including those of the Phoenicians, Greeks, Romans, Carthaginians, and Arabs — have targeted Corsica and Sardinia for strategic control of trade routes and to exploit metal and mineral resources. Both Corsicans and Sardinians are very tough, independent-minded people, traditionally shepherds and farmers, with a deep love for their gorgeous homeland. They have a legacy of family vendettas, ignited over the smallest slight, and sometimes lasting a century. The islands have been plagued in recent times by banditry and kidnappings.

Corsicans and Sardinians have a long tradition of allowing their animals to range free, and on the back roads drivers must take care to avoid goats, cows, donkeys, and pigs. This ancient and thrifty manner of maintaining livestock also provides the most flavorful and healthy produce, whether eggs, cheeses, or meat. The island pigs tend to be puny compared to massive domestic pigs raised under industrial conditions. Many of the Corsican free-range pigs mix with wild boars, called *cignali* in the local dialect. The pigs acquire distinctive boar features: bristles, straight tails, and lateral stripes on the young. These pigs with higher myoglobin coming from muscle use provide darker, richer meat. In fact, some studies suggest that the island boars are a product of re-feralization.

Even with interbreeding between free-range pigs and wild boars as they share the chestnut and oak groves, it is thought that almost half of the wild boars remain relatively pure. Like the pigs, the wild boars of Corsica and Sardinia are far smaller than mainland boars. Among the *Sus scrofa* species, only boars from the Ryukyu Islands in southern Japan are smaller. Given the fact that island donkeys, deer, and wild horses are also small, smaller boars are most likely a result of "insular dwarfism," a phenomenon that is reflected in the miniature domestic pigs of the islands through free-range husbandry and selection.

We planned only a three-day sojourn in Corsica and made hotel reservations in the small south central village of Quenza. We drove quickly down the eastern coast and west into the rugged mountainous central parklands. Even the national roads were small, winding through pine groves, heath land, and pastures, the craggy granite mountains always in view above. The roads were undoubtedly ancient trails that shepherds with their livestock had followed, transhumance bringing them to the coastal lowland pastures and then to high villages in summer.

On a curve where there was an entrance to a fire road, an entire family of free-range hogs had congregated. At first I thought they were wild boars, but when I got out of the car, expecting them all to flee into the woods, the opposite occurred. The whole group galloped toward me. As I tried to back away, I found myself surrounded by pigs on the road.

Traffic became jammed on one of the main arteries in the park as families abandoned their cars to take pictures of this scene. The vacationers fed the pigs whatever was at hand, even digging up ham sandwiches and chewing gum. The pigs seemed ecstatic with so much attention. Two out of the group had singled me out. While petting them, I could feel the coarse hair on their backs, and I noticed some stripes remaining on the flanks of the younger one. Their ears stood up as did their straight and tufted tails, and their snouts seemed longer than those of typical pigs — all characteristics of wild boars.

Mountain villages like Quenza, with granite buildings and meager economies, are not exactly brimming with easy charm. They have a more eccentric quality, with their mixture of old-timers — artisans, masons, and farmers — living side by side with late-arriving sculptors and painters enjoying the unfettered lifestyle. We settled in at Quenza's single hotel, the Auberge Sole e Monti, and took a walk, passing the one bourgeois house in the village, the lawn of which was dotted with whimsical sculptures of spirits carved out of the roots and trunks of oak trees. In the neighboring woods, we found extensive areas that had been excavated by wild boars.

Having the only good restaurant in the area, the *auberge* was already animated on our return and completely full by the time we entered the salon. Diners significantly increased the population of the village during the summer evenings. The restaurant, with its idiosyncratic décor of antique North African firearms, featured regional dishes, including fresh river trout, rabbit, and a wild boar *civet*. Mary and I both chose the *civet*, of course, remarkable for its dark, nearly black sauce (classically made with blood, but more often enhanced with dark chocolate), served with fresh pasta. The dish was superb.

Corsicans, the mountain people in particular, have a reputation for being reserved to the point of gruffness. The locals that we met in Quenza, however, were exactly the opposite. The convivial patron of the *auberge* was pleased that we had both chosen the *civet,* a house specialty. After lavishly complimenting the meal, Mary asked, "Was it blood in the sauce or chocolate that made the sauce so rich and velvety?"

"Madame, you know there would be no mystery if we gave away our secrets," he replied with a coy smile.

On our way to the southern coast and a visit to the Cauria Megaliths, Mary was keen on traversing the Alta Rocca, a region of Corsican vendettas and folk-hero bush bandits, and stopping at tiny Aullène, where the village church, Église Saint-Nicolas, housed a pulpit that was supported by wood-carved sea monsters emanating from a Moorish head. The town, shuttered up and without a soul on the streets, seemed to have only animals for residents. A brown cow sauntered down garden steps, past softly billowing laundry, while a black-and-white one meandered in the streets, looking into parked vans. Occasionally she let loose with a bronco kick to fend off an incorrigible German shepherd that persisted in annoying her.

Inside the church, we found three masons, the only people we saw in town, seated in a row, smoking filterless cigarettes where the pulpit should have stood. One said, "You came for this?" He pointed to the right side of the church where the carved pulpit had been moved. We glanced briefly at the carving, the strange Moor's head, the sea monsters twisting upward. Suddenly a hog, more boar than domestic pig, poked its head in the doorway and entered the church, startling us. That in turn startled the boar, which scrambled at top speed out to the road amid the cows. The austerity of Aullène was transformed by the whimsy of animals.

For years, we've been going to Sardinia, specifically to the town of Villasimius in the southeastern corner. Tuscany and Sicily may be richer in culture and cuisine, but we had developed a personal affinity for the strange island and always rent the same miniscule, but affordable, apartment over the Cala Caterina, with a view across the entire Golfo Degali Angeli to Monte Ascosu in the west.

The appeal of Sardinia is not just the silver-colored mountains, the spice and herb odors of the colorful brush *màcchia,* and the azure water. Sardinia has a funky lost-world atmosphere, particularly in the off-season. While Maremma may claim to be Italy's cowboy region, Sardinia feels like a spaghetti western, where the majority of the road signs have been ornamented with bullet holes and speckled with mini-buckshot galaxies. And as in Corsica, the wild boar provides the ultimate hunt.

Arriving in the north, either by Porte Torres or Golfo Aranci, we enjoy driving the narrow and twisting roads across passes and above breathtaking cliffs with valley and sea views in Gennargentu National Park. This time we stopped along Strada Nationale 125 to commune — as was becoming our habit — with free-range pigs.

No two pigs looked the same: they were striped and spotted, rich rust, deep chocolate, and uniform black. The youngest pigs were the most eager to greet us, raising some concern that sows might become protective. But the pigs were so good-natured that we could easily have rustled them if the spirit of banditry had suddenly seized us.

Wild boars are a cult animal in Sardinia. Even on New Year's Eve, the island's capital, Cagliari, has celebrated with boar festivals, a Sagra del Cinghiale. Throughout the year, boar festivals are held in villages along with celebrations of other meats, fish, mushrooms, fruits, wines, and cheeses. But the Sagra del Cinghiale is the most evocative festival, often associated with medieval themes or settings. Such culinary celebrations of boar take place throughout Italy.

Sardinians produce excellent boar sausages and dried filet and specialize in roasting boar. A classic island dish is *gnocchi Sardi* with wild boar. The dish uses traditional hand-scored gnocchi that the Sards call *malloreddus,* and the sauce, a *ragù* really, incorporates a rich array of vegetables: celery, carrots, onions, and tomatoes to go with the savor of juniper berries, bay leaf, garlic, and parsley. The characteristic flavor comes from the near-black, full-bodied Cannonau wine, the almost spicy native olive oil, and the island's pecorino cheese.

Boars living in the groves, orchards, and *màcchia* around Villasimius turn up the ground wherever they go. They live in protected natural areas just outside of town, but remain just as elusive as those in France. Because of the cult status of the Sardinian cinghiale and its different physique, I was keen to see one in the wild. My friend Amedeo, who grew up in southwestern Sardinia, offered to set me up with hunters, explaining that in Italy hunting involves a highly structured social system. Hunting groups often have a leader who chooses lieutenants, a position earned through experience and respect. The sport resembles a disciplined military operation.

I thanked Amedeo, but said that I'd rather just observe a Sardinian boar in the wild, at which point he began complaining about the boars that had eaten all of the potatoes he'd planted at his father-in-law's house in Nuoro. "What's the point of planting potatoes?" he groused. "They even got into the lettuce. It's useless. I'm just making fat boars."

Amedeo's wife was also an island native, but in north central Sardinia, she grew up with a different dialect. In Sardu Logudoresu, the language she heard, wild boar is called *porcràbu,* whereas in the south Amedeo heard, in Sardu Campidanesu, *sirboni* for boar.

I discovered by pure chance that behind a series of connected peaks called the Seven Brothers (Sette Fratelli), a nature preserve had been established in part by the World Wildlife Fund for the regeneration of the severely endangered Sardinian deer. The forest also provides a refuge for mouflon, golden eagles, and wild boar. We took an excursion through the cavernous river valleys between Muravera to Cagliari, marveling over mountain goats, mere specks, bleating to each other as they teetered on improbable hoof holds over vast precipices. At the highest point on our passage where rivers flowed east and west, a forest station with an entrance to the reserve appeared.

It was too late that first evening to enter the forest, but a sign alerted us to the protected animals. We continued on a road to a mountain crest topped by a stark tower built by the Neolithic Nuraghi people. A free-range stallion on a far hill warned us repeatedly away from his two mares. Someone had built a shack in the holm oaks and raised Sardinian wild boars. Black and silver with small compact bodies, they pressed up to the fence, deeply curious about us.

"They look like they just walked out of an Italian hairdresser. They are beautifully groomed," Mary said. She had been expecting disheveled, even scrawny little versions of our mud-adoring French boars. Sardinia was clean and dry, and so were its boars.

Still keen on seeing boars in the wild, we returned the following evening to walk the reserve as the sun began to set, the valleys already in shadow, the air fragrant with herbal odors, not a soul around. I thought we might at least see the mouflon, deer, and eagles indicated on the signs posted every half mile, but the park felt vacant. Though discouraged, I assured Mary we'd see a boar before we left the park. As a scientist, Mary is a staunch pragmatist, a devotee of "seeing is believing." But even she has accepted that the art of boar watching requires faith. She might explain it as the kind of faith that inspires vigilance and perseverance. Sure enough, a scrawny thigh-high creature with silver bristles climbed up the rocky hillside, stumbling and knocking rocks loose as she went, legs splaying. It appeared that boars, or at least this particular Sardinian boar, have no aptitude for negotiating rubble. She crossed in front of us and continued an arduous scramble up the hill.

Before leaving Sardinia, we prepared yet another picnic of roadside produce and bought a bottle of dark Cannonau to take on the "dog" ferry. The next morning we crossed the Pisan basin, through the tunnels of Ligura, and drove north over the Piedmont, exclaiming at the stunning views of Monte Bianco and the Massiccio del Monte Rosa. Our lunchtime destination was the Sagra Celta del Cinghiale, a wild boar festival that lasted two days in the tiny Italian village of Migiandone a couple of miles west of the shores of Lake Maggiori.

Arriving at the festivities, we found townspeople dressed in Celtic garb, and crude tents and banners bearing Celtic symbols. The men wore headbands and boar-tusk necklaces and acted out mock sword battles. Women in robes made rope and sewed leather helmets, while beautiful horses appeared with Celtic decorations.

Paying an entrance fee entitled us to a mug and access to five-gallon jugs of black wine distributed throughout the village, all equipped with pumps for a quick fill-up. The crowd mingled on village streets, carrying cups aloft like beggars. Even the children had mugs in hand, and also boar dolls under their arms. The central point of interest was the dining tents, of course, with their rows of tables and benches. Under one tent, five men were stirring separate cauldrons of polenta and wild boar *ragù* with oar-sized paddles. One could order *salsiccia di cinghiale in umido* or *cacciatorini de cinghiale*. Most boar festivals have men manning charcoal fires and whole boars on a *broche*, or ribs on a barbecue. In each case, men tend to cook for larger community events, one of the qualities noted about *un buon'uomo* in the Società del Cinghiale.

While clearly the *sagra* was designed to attract tourists and support commerce and church activities, the boar itself was honored with a photographic exhibit strung on a garden fence with flowering vines. The stunning shots captured boars swimming ponds, leaping brooks, nuzzling mountain snow, fending off dogs, twisting with a bullet wound in midair flight.

Drunken adolescents jostled and taunted each other while young children clutching their stuffed boars followed their parents past the dramatic boar photographs. All were oblivious to the actual majestic animal that inhabited the panorama of rugged alpine forests that rose around us.

Chapter Eleven

The Divine Beast

BOARS, MAMMOTHS, modern humans, and Neanderthals co-existed in the region where we have our country home. I hadn't thought about this until I walked into a nearby church obscured in scaffolding and masonry dust and saw an elaborate display of man-made stone artifacts spanning from the early Pleistocene era to the beginning of the Holocene. The village of Saint-Privé is only eight miles from us and three miles from the storied chateau of Saint-Fargeau, where some halls are so cluttered with boar- and deer-trophy legs that the walls resemble cuneiform tablets.

The Saint-Privé exhibition was meticulously arranged to show the technical evolution in tool making from the crudely chipped Lower Paleolithic artifacts to intricately hewn flint from the Mesolithic and early Neolithic periods. The caramel-colored flint, or *silex* in French, is a form of quartz so common in our region that our house is built from it. In the fields, you can find *silex* in rounded shapes reminiscent of Henry Moore sculptures. When flaked, it takes on a sharp, durable edge. The earliest Europeans utilized flint to make points, scrapers, knives, hammers, axes, awls, stakes, and hoes. The exhibition included tools to make tools: chipping stones and arrow-shaft files.

The entire collection came from farmland on a ridge less than three miles from the Saint-Privé church, and the owner, a thin man with a well-groomed beard and self-tinting glasses, stood authoritatively beside the exhibition he had assembled. This was André Huchet. The exhibition drew two other locals, who chatted with each other, leaving me the opportunity to ask Huchet how he began collecting his relics.

"It didn't happen right away," he responded. "I came here from the Orleans area in the 1970s, and I leased the farm over there that I now own. I always knew the earliest Europeans lived along the valley, and that the area was a major migration route for large animals. Then, in the 1980s, I started finding tools."

"Do you have your first find here?"

"It was this one." He picked up a milky gray, heart-shaped stone, with large cloven surfaces on both sides, and placed it in my palm. "When I saw this stone in the field," he said with satisfaction, "I knew it was exceptional."

The point was clearly intended for hunting large and often dangerous animals: aurochs, bison, stags, boars. Not far away is Arcy-sur-Cure, a major site with parietal and portable art as well as artifacts from both a Neanderthal and a modern *Homo sapiens* presence. At Soucy, another Paleolithic site in our department, excavations reveal that boars then as now were among the game animals hunted in our area.

Monsieur Huchet invited me to his home the following Sunday, and I was astonished to see that he had transformed the entire second floor of his farmhouse into a showcase for his finds. He had set up pedagogical charts and pictures showing animal-migration routes and Paleolithic sites with parietal art and artifacts. After a brief lecture on stone toolmaking, he showed me a comic book on the history of Burgundy. It pictured his younger self descending from a tractor and finding the triangular stone I'd held. The next frame shows Huchet hallucinating a stegosaurus, a brontosaurus, and a pterodactyl.

"I'm just a *petit paysan,* nothing but a farmer, but even I know that the periods of early man and the dinosaur don't coincide." Huchet's self-deprecating *"petit paysan"* had a bitter edge. His rich archaeological site and his important finds have received no recognition from the French scientific establishment because Huchet is not a degreed paleontologist and has not followed scientific procedures for marking and mapping his discoveries.

French academic snobbery is legendary. One of the most infamous examples was the sneering disrespect shown Don Marcelino Sanz de Sautuola after he and his nine-year-old daughter discovered the now-renowned cave drawings at Altamira. Sautuola was ridiculed and even accused of forgery. The snobbery here was twofold: not only was Sautuola dismissed as a fraud, but Paleolithic man was considered too "savage" to have produced such sophisticated renderings. Only after Sautuola's death did enough evidence accrue, paradoxically from Paleolithic finds in France, to force his critics to regret their condemnation.

When you see the Altamira animals, primarily bison in numerous positions and natural activities depending on the conformation of the stone, you almost have to sympathize with Sautuola's detractors: the paintings are nuanced, beautiful, and strangely modern. Altamira has a pair of images that are presumed to be boars among a swirl of bison. One image, which has been interpreted as one of the earliest attempts at animation, depicts what appears to be a boar with eight legs, suggesting motion.

I wanted to see the boars, even in facsimile, at Altamira and talked Mary into an impulsive 800-mile drive to the medieval town of Santillana del Mar in northern Spain. We broke up our drive with a night near the village Salies-de-Béarn. Legend has it that a mortally wounded boar in the Pyrénées-Atlantique region of France led its pursuers into a swamp. When the hunters finally found the animal, it was preserved in salt crystals, and upon salt mines and healing baths the village of Salies-de-Béarn was founded. The salt is used to cure hams in the region, including the famed jambon de Bayonne distributed throughout France. Later I would hear a similar tale. In Germany, a hunter shot a boar he had mistaken for an albino. It turned out that the boar had been frolicking in salt, the discovery of which led to the founding of Lüneburg. Honoring the legend, the town hall prominently displays a bone from the alleged "salt boar."

On Sunday, we arrived in Santillana del Mar and picnicked near a small, crowded beach between two dark, rocky points. The shoreline was rugged but very green, and thus appropriately named Costa Verde. Our plan was to visit Altamira the next morning and then drive into the rugged Picos de Europa mountain range.

Our hotel was situated on the edge of town, less than two miles from the famous cave and just across the street from a small zoo that we noticed first when we heard peculiar animal noises from it and saw storks circling and congregating in stripped treetops. Mary was unenthusiastic about visiting a run-down Spanish zoo, but ultimately she gave in and we found ourselves staring at listless Iberian boars along with scrawny wolves and bears lost in a diurnal coma. A beautiful Iberian lynx charged a tourist who was amusing his family by taunting it through protective glass. The animal looked far too noble and distinguished to be baited into zoo humiliations.

As solitary hunters, lynxes are not strong enough to prey on boars. But Iberian wolves are. They work in packs and target young or weak animals. Wolves have never been totally eradicated in Italy and Spain as they were in France, England, and other parts of Europe. Iberian wolves keep boar populations in check in the west central region of Spain.

We made reservations for the first tour at Altamira the following morning. Arriving at the site, one sees a low, boxy museum perched on a limestone ledge, overlooking green pastures that extend to the ocean. The museum is a state-of-the-art, interactive multimedia center dedicated to re-creating the local life of *Homo sapiens* during the Upper Paleolithic period. The displays show how stone tools were used for hunting, butchering, and preparing animal hides. Wild boars were of course included; in addition to meat and hides, they provided tusks for tools and ornaments.

Like Lascaux, Altamira is a facsimile. The general public, producing too much image-damaging carbon dioxide, is forbidden entry to the actual protected UNESCO World Heritage site. What Don Marcelino Sanz de Sautuola and his daughter discovered more than a century ago remains in darkness within the original cave created by drainage through a limestone fissure.

But even in facsimile, the "Sistine Chapel" of the Soutrean and Magdalenian periods is stunning, a swirling mass of beautifully rendered ochre and charcoal bison. I soon realized, however, that the boar images I'd come so far to see had been edited out. The animal map showed that each boar appears at the margins of the wheeling bison. Was it an artistic decision, maintaining an Aristotelian aesthetic sense of unity, or simply a financial one? You can't include everything.

We left Altamira to spend the remainder of the day in the snow-topped Picos de Europa. While browsing local produce for a Spanish-style picnic, we discovered that Cantabria and Asturias, the regions of Altamira and Picos, specialize in cheese making. The rocky foothill soil, the rain, and the fog from the sea combine to make suitable pastureland for sheep, goats, and cattle. Over the centuries, thousands of caves were dug in the hillsides to house small wheels of aging cheese; bats, spiders, and mice moved in on their own. Wild boars, *jabales* in Spanish, also share the foothills. In fact, while wolves, bears, and lynx are protected, part of the Picos is a hunting preserve and boars are among the prime game. Spain is a pork-obsessed culture, and *jabalí* is very common, especially in sausage form. Many of the Spanish stew recipes are similar to those of Italy and France, but the marinade — often Rioja, local herbs, and Spanish peppers — gives a distinctive regional flavor.

The Iglesia de Santa Maria de Lebena is a tenth-century stone church with warm yellow stone walls, simple lines, and terra-cotta roof, all dwarfed by the dramatic limestone peak of the Desfiladero de la Hermida. We chose the church grounds for a picnic, and sure enough, from the wall where we sat and ate we could see that boars had been rooting along the edge of the cemetery.

On the drive back, we visited Pech-Merle, where we gazed on the original animal renderings and abstract images, our imaginations transported millennia into the past. As at Altamira, contours of the limestone seemed to inspire the Paleolithic artists. In particular, a ragged limestone corner in the cave provided the outline of a horse's head and chest. Thus, the whole form of the horse was painted with another superimposed, both spotted with charcoal and a mixture of magnesium and barium oxides blown through a tube. Hands were comically outlined, and a large pike etched across the surface.

Among the 576 images there are mammoths, bison, horses, aurochs, ibex, reindeer, and a bear, but no boars. Why? Boar bones and tusks are found among the tools and debris at Paleolithic sites in Europe, yet wild boars are practically nonexistent in French parietal art, and there exist only a few examples in Spain. So why are boar images so rare? I traced studies of animal populations over the millennia, and clearly the wild boar was more prevalent during periods of warming, but still boar remains are a part of sites dating to Neanderthals and mammoths. It is thought that Neanderthals hunted boars not only with spears with fixed stone points but also with sharpened wooden stakes, something difficult to fathom. But the process for selecting animals for wall-art bestiaries remains a mystery.

While passing north into the Périgord and pondering questions of cave art, we learned that like their Paleolithic brethren, the contemporary French residents of the same region prize boar meat. In fact only thirty miles from Pech-Merle is one of the largest wild-boar farms in France: Les Sangliers de Mortemart. Not only can you enjoy a guided tour to see five hundred wild boars, but you can also take them, or parts of them, home with you in the form of pâté, *civet,* dried ham, bacon, and *enchaud périgourdin,* a boar filet with garlic. They even sell pure boar rillettes, something that, according to Bajon, our butcher, doesn't exist, since rillettes require fat.

Puzzled, I asked Mary, "How could this be? Pure boar rillettes."

"This is the region of the fattened duck, so why not the fattened boar, too?" she reasoned. Sure enough, Les Sangliers de Mortemart also raises and fattens ducks for their gastronomic boutique.

You can also buy whole, fresh marcassins all year around. They are sold at their living weight, but by law, the farm must eviscerate the animal before selling it as meat. Then you can customize your order and even take home the beautiful striped pelt.

On returning to Paris, I contacted the communications department at Altamira, asking how to acquire photographs of the two wild boars painted at the extremities of the swirls of bison. I was interested in the eight-legged boar that showed locomotion. These Altamira images, especially the one known as the "leaping boar," consistently appear in boar-hunting books and hunting-ranch publicity, accompanied by the opening statement that humans have hunted wild boar to provide for their families since the Stone Age.

To make sure that Altamira could clearly identify the images, I sent

Czech Brno Museum reproduction of the Altamira cave painting
thought to have been early animation of a boar.

photographs of the boar reproduction at Brno Museum in the Czech
Republic. A message arrived stating that the National Museum and
Research Centre of Altamira would gladly "lend" the "bison" images.
I was informed that, based on the research of L. G. Freeman, the Alta-
mira boars were no longer considered boars but bison, that horns had
been etched onto the eight-legged boar. Who's to say someone didn't
add the horns later like the fish image scratched across the horses at
Pech-Merle? Could Paleolithic graffiti be discounted?

After my initial disappointment about the morphing of Altamira's
boars into bison, I came across a wild-boar bas-relief dating back to
18,000 BC that had been excavated from a limestone shelter called the
Abris du Roc de Sers. It is displayed at the National Archaeology Museum in the prosperous Paris-region town of Saint-Germain-en-Laye.
The museum is housed in what was originally a feudal castle and later

transformed into an elegant chateau with a ballroom now filled with treasures from the beginning of civilization. No one seems to dispute that the head in the bas-relief is that of a boar, but the body resembles that of a bison, so the decision is to call it a rare composite animal. Facing the bas-relief was a display of animal fragments found at cave sites, including a well-preserved boar jaw sporting a tusk that avid hunters today would envy for a trophy.

While wild boar seemed to lack divine veneration during the Paleolithic period, the oldest known temple, Göbekli Tepe, dating to the debut of the Neolithic period, gave prominent attention to the boar. The ten-thousand-year-old temple located in Turkey's Kurdish country near the Syrian boarder features four circular complexes with configurations of T-shaped pillars. One complex is known as "the circle of boars" since six pillars portray wild boars with enormous heads and tusks in bas-relief. In addition, four boar sculptures were uncovered. Strangely, this earliest-known temple was used as a Neolithic animal refuse dump. The temple obscured the refuse pit until the mid-1990s, when archaeologists dug through the animal remains, including the bones of nearly a thousand boars.

Boars play an important iconographic role in numerous monuments and temples around the world. Some of the most stunning images are found among the carved reliefs at Taq-e Bostan in the Iranian Zargos range. The Indian maharajas relished boar hunting, particularly pig-sticking with spears six to ten feet long. Miniatures in gouache pigmented with gold and silver depict the turbaned royals on horseback, spearing boars or slashing at their backs with scimitars. Vishnu's avatar Varaha, a boar-god that saves the submerged world, is depicted in bas-relief and sculptures in Hindu temples and often appears in popular contemporary images. The boar also plays a significant role in Far Eastern cosmology. The Chinese zodiac includes twelve animal signs, the last being the boar. Japan has the Goo-Jinja boar shrine near Kyoto, commemorating the divine intervention of the three hundred guardian boars in saving the monarch. To worshippers, Goo-Jinga symbolizes safe journeys and rapid healing, reminiscent of Celtic beliefs. The first

Vishnu as Varaha, the wild boar avatar who rescues the world, painted in the
Punjab Hills (ca. 1700–1710). (© The Trustees of the British Museum)

Year of the Dog passes the baton to the Year of the Pig,
Russian State History Museum. (© Pyatakov Sergey/RIA NOVOSTI)

boars arrived in Hawaii from the Marquesas Islands in AD 400, thanks
to Polynesian voyagers and migrations. Now boars are wanted dead or
alive (mostly dead) for their crimes against agriculture and endangered
species. Hawaii has its own shape-shifting demigod, Kamapua'a —
literally, "hog-man" — that appears in indigenous art.

Boars are symbols of ferocity, fertility, abundance, light, and good
luck. The one true wild-boar temple is in Malaysia's Taiping, the Om
Sakthi Sri Jada Muneesvarar Alayam Hindu temple unpromisingly located behind a Tesco hypermarket. At 7:30 p.m., when the temple bell
tolls for evening prayer, up to eighty wild boars will filter out of Zenith
Park and onto the temple grounds, and locals and tourists arrive by the
dozens just for the opportunity to pet one. Legend has it that petting
these boars or rubbing money against them will bring various forms of
good fortune.

I am not immune to superstitions, as evidenced by my devotion to rubbing *Porcellino*'s nose every time I visit Florence. Through the ages, boars have represented prosperity, thus good luck, so petting or scratching a wild boar for good auspices when traveling and gambling may simply be an offshoot. Petting a live boar can get the adrenalin flowing, particularly when you are strongly advised against it. A boar can deliver a damaging bite, as Monsieur Delanoe will attest, but boars enjoy a good scratch on par with any cat or dog. Coincidentally, there is a nature park with a wild boar enclosure not far from Monsieur Huchet's artifact-laden farmland, and, as at Zenith Park, the boars rush to greet visitors.

Chapter Twelve

Beautiful Monsters Back Home

Z OOMING IN ON a satellite image of Matagorda, Texas, you see a complex convergence of water systems. The Colorado River, not to be confused with the western river with the same name, winds roughly south, skirting the Southwest Texas Nuclear Generating Station and its reservoir for the pressurized water reactors. The river then bends around the small gridlike town of Matagorda itself before finally culminating in an alluvial fan in Matagorda Bay. From space, the fan looks more like a green upside-down tree with swirls of yellow silt for branches.

Before arriving in the bay, the river transects the busy Gulf Intracoastal Waterway, trafficked by enormous barges transporting petroleum and chemical products. These barges pass through two locks on either side of a navigation channel that allows direct access from the river to the open waters of the Gulf of Mexico. The channel cuts through a narrow strip of shrubby land flanked by a system of bayous filled with crab traps: more than thirty miles of bay lie on one side of it and twenty on the other. At the mouth of the channel there is a state park and nature center, and two concrete jetties extending about a mile into the gulf. On the sand flats near the east jetty and the riverbank, I spent one Halloween night in what turned out, to my complete surprise, to be perfect wild-hog country.

My friend Bill Montgomery and I had talked for years about fishing for speckled trout and red drum together, a proposed outing mildly complicated by our living on separate continents. However, we managed to escape for two autumn days while I was visiting Texas. Based on Texas Parks and Wildlife fishing reports and Bill's judgment, we agreed on Matagorda at the last minute. Aside from being a gifted artist and naturalist, Bill is a passionate fisherman. Our timing was uncanny as I arrived in my small Kia rental car from Houston Airport directly behind Bill's camper, which was trailing an aluminum sled boat.

The east side of the channel is lined with houses on stilts and docks fitted out with high-powered lamps for attracting fish. The western bank is protected land, a part of the Coastal Barrier Resource System. Its distinguishing feature is the canebrake, shrubs, and reeds from which Matagorda derives its name: "fat brush" in Spanish. As soon as we launched the boat at a public ramp between a stand of common reed and a bait shack next to the Reef Lounge, a small, black wild pig emerged from the dense underbrush on the far bank and stood beside a small, dilapidated dock. The bank was heavily churned up and excavated in parts, with several wallows at the water's edge. The first pig was soon followed by three more, all about the size of those I'd seen in Corsica and Sardinia.

Boars began arriving via hidden paths, and Bill and I counted fourteen wild hogs grouping on the shore. A very large male appeared and headed straight for the well-used wallow on the riverbank, trailing several smaller wild pigs. The boar, light khaki color, turned broadside to us and lowered himself into the river mud.

The group had all the features of European wild boar: long snouts, furry erect ears, coarse, bristled hair down the spine, and straight tail with tuft. The large male had small tusks. But their torsos were decidedly more cylindrical, with less muscular bulk about the shoulders, a morphology indicating that they were common Texas feral hogs with a representation of European wild boar in their genes. While they seemed habituated to human commerce on the channel, they were cautious enough to melt back into the shrubbery as we approached their shore. Bill was convinced they were being fed in preparation for hunting. Why else would they make themselves so evident?

The wild pigs are a part of an elaborate ecosystem. At first, Matagorda gives the impression of an austere, almost grim landscape: dead flat with grayish silted waterways and reed-filled marshes extending as far as you can see. But it doesn't take long to realize that the area is teeming with wildlife. Within an hour, pelicans, kingfishers, curlews, plovers, and falcons may all appear. The area is on the migratory route of numerous bird species. There are raccoons, coyotes, and alligators on the banks. Blue crabs scavenge the murky shallows. Even a porpoise approached us on the river.

Later that night, we set up camp near the mouth of the channel and put out fishing lines on a starless Halloween night. Two pickups arrived carrying high-spirited groups of Nicaraguan immigrants with casting nets. Other fisherman began arriving, too, the most surrealistic being a man wading with three-foot, battery-powered fluorescent tubes that projected green light on the shallows for jigging flounder. The men with casting nets quickly loaded pails with an impressive variety of fish, shrimp, and crabs. Flashlights darted over the shallows and beach, and the Nicaraguans shouted, "You should do like us!" They discarded little, regardless of the juvenile size of most of their flapping or crawling catch. For wild pigs, it was a wetland paradise with limitless dining possibilities.

Wild boars are known to thrive in coastal areas, swimming in estuaries, bays, and even the open ocean for two miles or more. In *La Chasse illustrée* (1872), a boar is pictured dramatically climbing onto, and nearly swamping, an open boat containing four panicked men, two of whom have weapons poised. Boars frequent shorelines in places as diverse as Morocco and Malaya.

In coastal Texas, they are a drain on food supplies for all animals since they are omnivores. On land, they forage for fungi, grapes, and acorns, and they chew up sprouts or dig bulbs. In the ponds and along the river's edge, they patrol the shallows eating submerged vegetation and cattail roots. Scouring the beach, they consume fish, crabs, eggs from nesting waterbirds, ribbon snakes, and algae. They have been known to dig clams.

That evening we stopped off at a convenience store to pick up some supplies. The clerk was a garrulous type, and when he heard of my interest in boars, he offered the tale of a recent deer hunt. Instead of the dream multipointed stag appearing before him, a crazed boar showed up, and, contrary to a boar's natural inclination to disappear, this one didn't: he charged the hunter. "I swear, this boar tore through that goddamn deer blind like a train," he said. "I had to take to the nearest tree."

A boar destroying a deer blind was implausible enough, but picturing this guy hefting his enormous girth into a tree without magical intervention was impossible. Still, whether in Europe or America, boars seem to inspire far-fetched scenarios. Not the least of these appears in *Don Quixote*. Sancho Panza, beholding a boar "gnashing its teeth and tusks, and spraying foam from its mouth," abandons the Duke and Duchess, the Don, and even his trusty mule, Dapple, and scrambles up an oak tree. In classic cartoon manner, the branch breaks, and as he plummets to earth, he becomes snagged on a different branch, leaving him suspended and shrieking for help.

Given that Texas has a feral pig population of 2 million and counting, it's no surprise that residents are busy generating boar lore. In a 2007 *Los Angeles Times* article titled "Wild Pigs Are Winning the Texas Boar War," a Texas boar-buster named Tommy Stroud is quoted as saying: "The hog is the poor man's grizzly.... If you shoot at a hog, you'd better shoot straight, because if you don't kill it, he might try and kill you."

One of the first movies my mother took me to as a kid was Vincente Minnelli's *Home from the Hill,* based on William Humphrey's eponymous novel. An East Texas boar hunt is portrayed as the ultimate rite of passage into manhood. Robert Mitchum, playing the tyrannical land baron Wade Hunnicutt, explains the ferocity of a cornered wild boar to his "mossy green," eager-to-prove-himself son, Theron, played by George Hamilton:

> The minute he sees you, he's gonna charge you. He'll rip right through those dogs to get at you. By the look of him and the size of him, you'd think he's bound to be slow. Don't you believe it. He's one of the fastest

things that moves. Don't aim for the head, too thick. Aim for the snout, you ought to hit the heart.... Make that first shot count. Because that's the last one you're likely to get. One of those brutes can keep going with a 30-30 bullet in his heart and still hit you hard enough to kill you.

The script provides more drama by straying from Humphrey's original text in which Hunnicutt advises, "Stand by a tree with some low limbs and throw the gun away from you and start climbing the second you pull the trigger."

I never forgot the first hunting dog being catapulted ten feet in the air, the second dying of exhaustion, and the third surviving a dreadful thrashing. Confronted with a charging boar, Theron manages to squeeze off the perfect shot just in time to save his own skin and earn the esteem of his diabolical father and the gratitude of the land-lease farmers and their families.

The images of the fearsome boar stuck with me for decades, though it turned out Minnelli had undoubtedly used an enormous trained domestic pig coated in black, with artificial tusks attached. What did I know? In the novel, Theron cuts off a trophy tail that is indicative of a domestic pig: "with his pocketknife he sliced off the corkscrew tail."

Growing up in boarless New England, I associated wild hogs with Texas, Arkansas, Louisiana, and Mississippi. Interestingly, René-Robert Cavalier, Sieur de La Salle, who explored the Mississippi basin and laid claim to it for France, is credited with bringing the first swine to Texas. La Salle's last expedition, aimed at establishing a French colony on the Gulf coast, experienced difficulty from the beginning. He left France with four ships and three hundred colonists. Pirates managed to appropriate one ship, and soon after another sank while entering the inlet to Matagorda Bay. A third ship ran aground, finally obliging La Salle to set up a fort inland in 1685. Among the supplies, he had apparently brought swine from the West Indies. While the human inhabitants of the fort would succumb within two years to smallpox and massacres by the Karankawa Indians, some of the hogs may have survived and escaped.

Fake wild boar as film prop: Mickey Rooney in *Pulp*.
(Collection of John Baxter)

Even before La Salle, however, explorers and colonists had transported swine to the Americas for sustenance. Although Columbus introduced them to the West Indies, it was Hernando de Soto who first
imported swine from Cuba to what would become the continental
United States. After de Soto left his modest beginnings behind in western Spain and joined Pizarro in his conquests and exploits in Central
and South America, he was named governor of Cuba, where he imported and propagated European swine. In 1539, he arrived in Florida
with a flotilla of nine ships, and among the armaments and supplies he
brought with him were two hundred hogs. De Soto may have perished,
but the ranks of these swine would swell eventually to seven hundred.
Many of the animals were distributed to de Soto's men and possibly
to Indians, but many others set out on their own into the marshes and
forests.

While explorers, conquistadores, and missionaries brought swine to the Americas, it was the hog-raising practices of the early settlers that contributed most to the burgeoning ranks of European swine. Lively scavengers, hogs were branded and allowed to roam freely and proliferate while requiring little of the farmer in the way of feed. These were the same free-range practices Mary and I had seen in Corsica and Sardinia, and those swine provided quality meat. In the weeks before butchering, farmers in the Americas would provide New World corn to fatten pigs and keep them near the homestead. Certain settlements were obliged to raise pickets and gates, not so much to keep hogs from escaping as to keep their rapidly increasing population out of the streets. Processed corn, known as hominy, became a signature staple of the South, especially during the slavery era, as it provided high-energy, low-cost food. Hominy was often served with pork. European swine played a noteworthy role in nourishing the nascent colonies and later the homesteaders: even so, a significant number slipped away and eventually became a feral nuisance.

The so-called Russian boar arrived in the United States with the advent of hunting reserves and the desire to harvest trophies of pure-bred species, an enterprise that continues to this day. The story of wild boars arriving in North Carolina serves as a good example for what has occurred in Texas and elsewhere. At the end of the nineteenth and the beginning of the twentieth centuries, the new capitalist aristocracy, the tycoons, created a version of Old World hunting recreation. While cabins in the Great Smoky Mountains hardly rivaled Chambord and its noble hunting forest, the fenced-in reserves stocked with purebred boar offered a gripping experience for leisured adventure seekers.

In 1908, with the guidance of George Gordon Moore, a savvy American securities investor, an English company purchased 100,000 acres of prime timberland in Graham County, North Carolina, including a mountain on the Tennessee border called Hooper Bald. In 1909, Moore leased game rights to create a hunting preserve, and soon after he had a twenty-mile road cut to the mountain to provide access to the nearest town with a railroad. Cabins were built and fencing installed. Moore introduced buffalo and elk, and then added forty bears purchased from zoos. The bears found little difficulty escaping, but they were so habituated to captivity they came right back for food.

In a letter fifty years later, Moore describes discovering wild boar through Walter Winans, who was a British Olympic gold medalist in shooting and a passionate boar hunter.

> I received an invitation from Winans to spend the weekend with him. This was the first time I ever heard anything about wild boar. He had his own boar hunting forest in Belgium. He was so enthusiastic I decided to add boar to my Graham County collection. He gave me the name of his dealer in Berlin. I wrote this man for the price on three boar and nine sow, the biggest and toughest he could find anywhere. He gave me his price, I paid it. He said they were from the Ural mountains of Russia. In due time they arrived at Andrews. Within a couple of years they had taken over the mountain; wild boar always have the initiative. You can never tell whether they run away from you or run at you, all the action any hunter wants.

Like the bears before them, boars found it easy to burrow under or wriggle through the fencing. They reproduced rapidly even as they were hunted at the reserve, and the population increased to nearly a hundred in ten years. Hunters with dogs simply succeeded in chasing the Russian boars out of the enclosure into southern Appalachia, where they are still multiplying and mixing with feral hogs.

Moore's letter was addressed to Stuyvesant Fish, who had inquired into how boars had come to populate the Carmel Valley area. The Fish family owned the Palo Corona Ranch, which in 2004 was acquired by the California Nature Conservancy and the Big Sur Land Trust and rechristened the Palo Corona Regional Park. Moore replied that he simply repeated his successful North Carolina boar-breeding experiment on his California ranch, using three boars and nine sows from North Carolina as his foundation stock.

As on Hooper Bald, the boars in Carmel Valley reproduced and readily escaped to enjoy the fruits of the seaside mountains and neighboring ranches, including that of Randolph Hearst, where he had constructed his famous castle. The boars were not always appreciated, not just for their disagreeable habits of tilling the grounds and bursting through fencing, thus liberating livestock and fowl. In 1965, they were responsible for transmitting bovine tuberculosis to the Hearst cattle herds.

The Monterey boars would make their way into the California poet Robinson Jeffers's poetry as here in "The Stars Go over the Lonely Ocean":

> "Keep clear of the dupes that talk democracy
> And the dogs that talk revolution,
> Drunk with talk, liars and believers.
> I believe in my tusks.
> Long live freedom and damn the ideologies,"
> Said the gamey black-maned boar
> Tusking the turf on Mal Paso Mountain.

Before coming to Europe, the closest I'd ever been to a boar in the wild, at least to my knowledge, was while camping with friends at the Andrew Molera State Park, the region of Jeffers's Tor House, which he built himself, and the Hearst Ranch, now also a park. It was a fairly typical camping experience: steady rain, fog rolling in from the sea, and sleeping bags that felt like cold mashed potatoes. However, a group of wild pigs woke us. We knew that Russians boars lived in the park. Boar tracks circled our campsite in the river meadow and formed a path to the sea along the Big Sur River.

That night I learned that few animals can compel the human imagination and emotions like the "poor man's grizzly," and the United States is no laggard in extremes. George Gordon Moore provides a telling example: "The biggest boar we ever killed on the ranch, when hung, measured 9 ft. from tip to tip. The skin on his neck was three inches thick; eleven bullets were found which over the years had been imbedded in the fat."

The boar Moore describes reminded me of a photo taken on June 17, 2004, near Alapaha, Georgia, that clicked in the national, even international, psyche obsessed with *Jaws,* Bigfoot, and the Loch Ness Monster. A good-looking hunting guide, thirty-one-year-old Chris Griffin, posed in a pit dug on the River Oak Plantation. Looming next to him was an enormous beast, which he had killed with a single shot. It was strung by its hind legs and seems to float over the pit since the backhoe suspending it is out of the frame. The boar's brown matted bristles matched the rich color of the Georgia soil. Griffin and property owner Ken Holyoak claimed the animal was a twelve-foot, 1,000-pound wild hog with tusks nearly a foot long.

When the photo was taken, Holyoak and Griffin were in the process of burying the monster. What else could they do with meat that was too gamey to eat and an animal, given its size, too expensive and unwieldy to stuff? Once Holyoak posted the photograph on the Web, an Internet frenzy followed, raising one stark question: "Is that thing real?" This wild pig would be dubbed Hogzilla, and worldwide news agencies, forever ravenous for wacky stories, spread the legend and at the same time amplified doubts. Griffin was for a short time a late-night show celebrity, and parades in Alapaha would feature a Hogzilla float and regalia. Alapaha was suddenly on the map.

National Geographic, with their television film crew and animal experts, exhumed Hogzilla and broadcast to the world that the photo was not a hoax and that, indeed, the animal was "a freak of nature," as the producer put it. However, they conceded that the pig could only have been eight hundred pounds and no more than eight feet long, sparking a whole new controversy about how much size had dissipated through subterranean decay or how long Hogzilla measured from snout to hind hoof as opposed to snout to rump.

So where does this place George Moore's nine-foot boar with eleven bullets lodged in its fat? The eleven bullets are understandable. It took French police thirty shots to subdue a boar that wandered into a department store, terrorizing last-minute Christmas shoppers; and German police emptied their weapons to no avail into a boar paying a visit to a liquor store.

Plenty of boar monsters have been created through the ages. Twrch

Trwyth, in Welsh myth, was known as "the greatest fighter boar-hog in medieval tradition." The potent creature leads the young hunter Culhwch, aided by his cousin King Arthur, on a complex symbolic quest to win his bride. Australians produced the horror film *Razorback,* in which a monster hog goes on a killing spree in the Outback. For the film writers of *The Legend of Hogzilla,* vaguely based on Chris Griffin's story, shooting a "freak of nature" wouldn't be enough for box-office viability; Hogzilla had to murder somebody to warrant vengeance. The writers decided it should be Griffin's wife.

Why was Hogzilla killed in the first place? Many have asked this question since "the freak of nature" was buried. Michael Pollan, in *The Omnivore's Dilemma,* struggles with this very question after he manages to shoot a respectably large feral hog in Southern California as a part of a planned hunter-gatherers' dinner. His hunting guide and friend Angelo Garro photographed Pollan with his sow, blood pooling next to him. The unrestrained pride captured in his own smile appalls Pollan only hours later and catapults him into soul searching:

> I couldn't for the life of me explain what could have inspired such a mad grin, it seemed so distant and alien from me now. If I didn't know better I would have said that the man in the picture was drunk. And perhaps he was, captured in the throes of some sort of Dionysian intoxication, the "blood lust" that Ortega says will sometimes overtake the successful hunter. And what was I so proud of, anyway? I'd killed a pig with a gun, big deal.

Mary and I often consider this same question about eating meat: one can't accept the pleasure of it without accepting the moral ambiguity. Pollan provides a humane death with one well-placed shot, the critical goal of the responsible hunter. The ambiguity he grapples with involves the pleasure of killing.

In his *New Yorker* article "Hogs Wild," Ian Frazier describes his own Georgia hog hunt not far from Apalaha and expresses decided relief that he had seen a hog in its natural habitat without its being shot. However, in his description of the Ocmulgee Wild Hog Festival, we quickly see that his subject has led him to a rural dog-hog rodeo in the form of a baying competition. In attendance were "dog guys," passionate hog hunters who get to show off the skills of their curs and pit bulls at the baying event. Of course, the critical challenge for them is the actual hunt: to run down a hog with dogs and then engage it, preferably in hand-to-hoof combat, and quite often using only a knife to subdue it.

It appears that boars are more suitable for knife hunting than are deer or coyotes. Reserves in Florida, Texas, and Hawaii enthusiastically promote this special "thrill." There is an assortment of knife-hunting videos shot with shoulder-hoisted camera so the viewer experiences vicariously the sensation of dashing through understory with knife in hand. Videos of this type have been dubbed "hunting porn."

A self-proclaimed master knife hunter reported to the *Houston Press News*, "It's an adrenaline rush.... It's addicting." Pictures posted on the Web are reminiscent of the one that struck Pollan with sudden shame: men and boys, grinning broadly, brandishing bloody knives above the vanquished hog. Some boast of accomplishing the task with a mere pocketknife.

With animal-rights activists supported by Harvard lawyers arguing for "personhood" status for animals and protection under the law, one can easily get caught up in the moral quandary over twenty-first-century hunting. Still, Americans are faced with the inexorable population growth and territorial expansion of wild boars, feral pigs, and hybrids. They are found in at least half of the fifty-two states. Damage to the environment and crops is great enough to prompt costly abatement programs.

A Texas ranch owner committed to environmental responsibility took Mary and me to dinner in Paris. Having heard of my interest, he had been eager to talk about boar hunts on his ranch. He invited me to a barbecue if I had time on my next trip to Texas. "These boys fly in with helicopters and shoot the hogs with automatic weapons," the rancher told us, seeming untroubled by the idea. "It helps control the boar populations on the ranch. They radio in the kill locations. The boar meat is processed and shipped to Germany. They love it over there. Do you know it sells for sixteen dollars a pound?"

German chancellor Angela Merkel and U.S. president George W. Bush at a
boar barbecue in Trinwillershagen, Germany. (© Mandel Ngan/AFP)

Germans and many Americans may enjoy eating boar, but meat
consumption is not a viable means of controlling populations. Mike
Bodenchuk, Texas director of USDA's Wildlife Services, is often called
on to comment on animal outlaws, including wild boar hybrids and
feral pigs. Asked about the consumer value of boar meat as a factor in
controlling Texas wild-hog populations, he responded, "Do the math:
When you have 2 million pigs having three litters every two years, you're
not going to eat your way out of this." The response is hardly a surprise,
coming from an official coordinating a million-dollar hog-abatement
program that puts helicopters and assault rifles to work against what
he considers "an environmental train wreck."

Members of the Texas Predator Posse boast of killing up to a hundred
hogs at a time using either an AR-15 or an AK-47 with 75-round ammo
drums. What one may lose in terms of the clean shot can be made up
with abundance. The films of helicopter hog hunts resemble a video

game, the sound and downdraft flushing black boar in a panic from one set of bushes to the next, meanwhile affording numerous opportunities to get a shot. Helicopter platform hunting is embraced by many farmers and landholders as an effective means of controlling hog damage.

Hog hunters come from all walks of life — law, business, professional sports, agriculture, and even veterinary medicine. The majority of hunters are responsible people, and most would profess both understanding and respect for wild animals and an active passion for conserving nature. When it comes to wild boar, Texas Parks and Wildlife wardens couldn't encourage hunting enough. As in France, where world dignitaries frequent the presidential hunting reserve at Chambord, public figures often arrive in Texas for a hunt.

Still, when it comes to boars and feral pigs, American hunting attracts a good deal of negative attention in the media and elsewhere. One senses another underlying element: "us against them." The *Los Angeles Times* profiled Joe Padock, aka the "Dehoginator," who claims to have a "vendetta" against hogs and who engages in nighttime Special Forces–type action to eradicate feral hogs on Texas farms and ranches. Still, feral hogs and wild boars garner little sympathy. Ninety percent of Texas has a hog problem and experts predict that despite widespread trapping, helicopter shoots, and the likes of the "Dehoginator," the population will continue to increase rapidly.

Nevertheless, nature centers on the Texas coast concede that boars are a main public attraction. The first time I saw them, I couldn't help anthropomorphize them myself as quintessential American outlaws, breaking out of the demeaning ranks of domestic animal and "referalizing" as Darwin described. They are a tribe of their own.

I once again had been boating with Bill but this time on rush-filled shallows of Somerville Reservoir and then up the well-hidden Yegua Creek. We anchored the boat for lunch at a tight bend in the creek where the confluence with a small tributary formed a calm pool. We heard rustling on the rise beside us and then the low grunts of typical hog discourse. We had only to wait a moment for a good-sized brown hog, the matriarch, to break cover. She stared down at us, but we only caught glimpses of the others, though we heard them trundling through the grasses and overhanging branches. This is their cautious system: the brown hog, sentinel for the sounder, needing only to give the signal and they would all vanish in an instant. She would never know it is we who are defending ourselves against her kind, monsters of our own making.

Chapter Thirteen

Fête du Sanglier

J EAN-MARIE BOISGIBAULT arrived at our door with his wife, Evelyne, on a cool but bright Sunday in November, when the air is rich with the odor of damp chestnut leaves on the place de l'Église. Jean-Marie, a sturdy, clean-shaven man, came to deliver a fully prepared, neatly wrapped wild boar rib roast as a gift. We couldn't have been the only recipients of such gifts. Ribs, shoulders, loins, and thighs were probably distributed throughout the villages given the army of hunters in our area.

The boar meat hardly differed from a pork rib roast straight from the butcher except that the flesh was a richer red like lamb. Almost a year had passed since Monsieur Delanoe had dropped half a boar in a black garbage sack on my lap, removing the comfortable gap between the actual beast and the meat that we would eat. But this time, Jean-Marie spared us any concerns about butchering, although by then Mary and I considered ourselves better equipped, if not in skills then at least in psychic fortitude, to deal with a bloody animal carcass.

Jean-Marie wore a light blue sweater and jeans and was making casual social rounds. He was a muscular man, balding, in his fifties, owner of a small roofing and masonry company in the neighboring village of Dammarie-sur-Loing. He renovated centuries-old houses and chateaux, notoriously struggling against dilapidation. Our house was one of these; Jean-Marie and his crew helped us bring it back to life. His profession is grueling, making days off precious, to be spent with family and friends, or out hunting in the fields and copses or fishing the numerous rivers.

On occasion, we'd see Evelyne, a blonde with serene brown eyes, sitting quietly in their Renault Kangoo minivan while Jean-Marie hunted in a nearby copse. She was painting miniatures on canvas: flowers, birds, game animals, and landscapes. Over the years, we had received greeting cards with her drawings of local animals, including sangliers. The Boisgibaults were fully occupied with their contrasting diversions. Evelyne rendered animals in imaginative tranquility, and Jean-Marie pursued them amid the tumult of dogs, gunfire, adrenalin-filled horn blasts, and men shouting to each other through the trees. "Don't go near those woods," Evelyne would warn us. "You could get your head blown off."

On receiving his gift, I asked Jean-Marie, "Did you shoot the boar yourself?" He hedged, answering only, "Eh ben." He was reluctant to discuss the kill, knowing we weren't keen on the sport but enjoyed game meat. He did respond when I asked where the boar had been hunted. "Pas loin. In the woods along the road to Breteau."

This is the area where I had spent nights looking for boars either by the three lakes and the isolated chateau with limestone blocks forming the dam or by a former railroad station marooned in the trees. I'd see them in groups or as single black shapes against the dark fields. My pseudo-spiritual wanderings at 3 a.m. may have led me to the very same wild boars that would show up on my dinner plate.

Jean-Marie and Evelyne didn't stay long, wanting mainly to deliver the piece of meat and continue their social rounds. Their pint-sized Jack Russell terrier watched us intently from the passenger window of their minivan. No doubt he would root out a boar if given the chance since Jack Russells have neither a sense of proportion nor lack of bravado. On parting, Evelyne offered, "I have recipes. Call if you'd like to have them."

Mary and I inspected the rib roast, trying to judge the weight and quality of the meat the way our butcher Monsieur Bajon might. The roast may well have come from one of the animals I had observed, but can meat eaters bemoan an animal's death? Can we mix pleasure with regret? The answer, obviously, is yes. But as Goethe writes in *Faust:* "There is nothing more absurd than a devil in despair." On a strictly practical level, wild boar is one of the healthiest meats you can consume if it is handled and cooked properly, and according to wildlife managers and scientists alike, you can pat yourself on the back for doing the environment and farmers a big favor.

Ultimately, one either becomes a vegetarian and avoids seeing himself as a "burial place" for God's creatures, as Leonardo da Vinci, a vegetarian, put it, or expresses sentimental indebtedness and celebrates the animal as the Gauls did. Caught up in the wonder of our latest gift of boar meat, I decided to honor the animal by organizing a dinner with a few close friends and began to ponder recipes — ones that I had received from cookbook writers and others that I found in French texts. With Mary listening and commenting, I read out the recipes that seemed most suited to ribs.

Côtes de sanglier à la Saint-Hubert is a classic. It refers to Saint-Hubert, who, while truant from Sunday mass to indulge his passion for hunting, had a vision of Christ on the cross between the antlers of a stag. A voice that accompanied his vision gave him the option of assuming the holy life or heading straight to hell. Understandably opting for the former, he became the patron saint of hunters and foresters, and the French invoke his name for dishes that include the flavors of the forest with chanterelle mushrooms, currants, and juniper. The Saint-Hubert sanglier dish even uses the throat of the boar and *crépinettes* derived from pig stomach. We were tempted by a refined honey and ginger dish, *carré de sanglier au miel et au gingembre.* I also came across the invention of chef Édourard Loubet: *Cuite dans son foin et relevée à la coriandre, côte de sanglier au gros sel, ses olives vertes et limaçons,* a dish that includes both olives and snails.

As soon as we settled on one dish, an ensuing recipe seduced us, including ones that required different cuts and fruits: *filet mignon de sanglier, pommes et mirabelles* (boar filet with apples and plums); *sanglier aux airelles et poires pochées* (boar with cranberries and poached pears); and *sanglier aux pêches de vigne et au cassis* (boar with peaches and currants). Rich boar meat is synergistic with fruits, honey, berries, chestnuts, mushrooms, vinegars, cognac, cider, and wine.

Our indecisiveness and curiosity finally led Mary to suggest, "Why don't we just have a wild-boar potluck? We could invite more friends. And they'd bring different dishes to try out. We would need more boar meat, but that shouldn't be so difficult to find."

The originality of a boar potluck appealed to me, although the question arose: Who among our friends would be willing not just to prepare an unusual dish but also to eat multiple boar dishes in succession? Each preparation included fruits, a starch, and vegetable side dishes. When we proposed the boar potluck, our friends predictably asked, "Are you serious?" But when we assured them we were, they couldn't resist the novelty of the idea, and our plan for a fête du sanglier rapidly organized itself into a feast for twelve guests and four different boar dishes based on our friends' culinary whims. My mother volunteered hors d'oeuvres and desserts.

Our volunteer cooks were our physician friends Laurent and Catherine, and Mary's colleague at the Pasteur Institute Jean-Michel, who had restored a country house just to the north of us. An old family friend Leonilda, a lively Italian American, who along with her British husband had bought a home in our village, wouldn't miss such an eccentric soirée. Naturally, Mary and I would contribute a dish as well.

Even a makeshift fête du sanglier required music. I coaxed Leonilda and Mary into opening the evening with a series of short piano and cello duets — our substitution for the traditional horns of the *battue de prestige,* or Celtic songs with flutes, harps, and drums. The concert would be followed by apéritifs, Vitteaut-Albert *crémant de Bourgogne,* and then the cooks would go to work with final preparations.

Our fête had the makings of a friendly cook-off. Wild boar festivals often include wild-hog cooking competitions, sometimes even for fund-raisers. While cooking contests conjure up images of Norman Rockwell–like characters entering their concoctions at the country fair, they can also become mass entertainment. World-famous chefs compete on television.

One of the pinnacles of boar-cooking competitions took place on the Food Network's *Iron Chef America,* a TV cooking program based on a very popular Japanese series called *Iron Chef.* The iron chefs in both the original Japanese and American versions are deemed "the invincible men of culinary skills," often experts in a particular genre of cooking. The program pits a resident iron chef against challenger chef in the "Kitchen Stadium," a studio setting to compete at making five dishes based on a theme ingredient within an hour. The host's hyperbolic commentary provides culinary drama on a par with *Monday Night Football.* The judges determine which chef "best expressed the unique qualities" of the preselected ingredient.

For the program featuring wild boar, the chefs David Bull and Bobby Flay, along with two assistants, each cooked five dishes, having been allowed only boar stock as an ingredient prepared in advance. The dishes were sophisticated and imaginative. David Bull's menu included wild boar "bacon" with garlic risotto, chive emulsion, caraway molasses glaze; and roasted boar loin with black truffle grits, braised fennel, sage brown butter. Bobby Flay came up with molasses braised wild boar with sweet potato polenta; and "Wild Boar Two Ways," boar poached in duck fat and back ribs with pomegranate glaze.

The menus of *Iron Chef America* were inspirational to us. Mary and I wanted to tackle a wild-boar preparation that came from outside the European sphere. One of the joys of researching recipes is appreciating how interwoven culture and food are. I landed on a traditional Japanese hot-pot dish called *botan nabe* that intrigued me since it almost comically addressed the meat-eater/vegetarian paradox.

In the fifth century, Chinese Buddhists' traditions were imported to Japan and soon took hold. Early emperors established strong taboos against the consumption of meat. At first, wild boar, or *inoshishi,* along with deer were exempt, but then all animals including fish were decreed off-limits for cuisine. If the unseemliness of eating meat weren't deterrent enough in the Buddhist society, potential execution surely made citizens think twice. Under these conditions, the Japanese wild boar flourished in more remote areas and was known as *yamakujira,* "whale of the mountain forest." Boars only had to contend with wolves, which in the old days enjoyed godlike status with the monks. Shinto shrines had been erected to honor wolves, and wolf talismans were also offered to farmers as supernatural protection against boars damaging precious crops.

During the Edo period, 1603 to 1867, wild boar began to appear mysteriously in a hot-pot dish called *botan nabe*. *Nabe* is literally a pot in which a broth is heated for cooking vegetables (and meat when allowed) at the table. *Botan* is a peony. To get around taboos, the Japanese monks would name various meats after plants and flowers, symbolically transmuting the forbidden flesh into flora. Boar, with its bright color, was carefully sliced to resemble peony (*botan*) petals, and thus a monk was spiritually consuming a flower. A friend who taught for many years in Japan explained to me that in Japanese culture, manipulating appearances is considered a high art.

Around Edo-period settlements, archaeologists have unearthed animal bones, the majority of which are from wild boar. The Edo period was followed by Meiji Restoration in 1868, precipitated, in part, by the impetuous arrival of Commodore Perry and his famous black steamships, leading to the opening of Japan to Western influence. With the imperial government reinstalled, meat found its way back into Japanese cuisine, and the last wolf on the islands was shot in 1896 (or so it was thought). Meanwhile wild boars flourished, overpopulating some areas and making nuisances of themselves to this day.

Though Japanese cuisine appears simple, it relies on a mania for high-quality, fresh ingredients and esthetic presentation. Flavors are kept intact and in equilibrium. *Botan nabe* is prepared at the beginning of November, when cold weather moves in and the wild boars have fattened on their autumn bounty supplemented with nocturnal raids on crops and country gardens. Often wild boars are raised and fattened for special *shishiniku*. While boar meat is generally lean, the fattened *shishiniku* remains flavorful even if left in the boiling broth for a long time.

I had enjoyed hot-pot dishes before in restaurants, but never *botan nabe*. This cold-weather specialty of Kyoto had yet to find its way to Paris. Nevertheless, I planned to try it out on our friends, and my first challenge was finding an authentic recipe that I could make sense of.

After making a compilation of several, I turned to the problem of tracking down ingredients.

Recognizing *udon* noodles and shiitake and enoki mushrooms posed no difficulty. However, common food terms for the Japanese — *konnyaku, shimeji, konbu, shungiku,* and *sanshō* — appeared only in characters in the Asian food market nearest me in Paris. In addition, the recipe asked for boar liver, a special red miso paste for *botan nabe,* and *gobo,* Japanese burdock root.

At the market, I begged the assistance of two women packaging fresh vegetables. They were all Vietnamese and baffled by my French pronunciation of Japanese products. Their solution was to shake their heads and foist me off on someone else until the chain of responsibility led me to the patron.

"Do you have any *sanshō*?" I wrote *sanshō* out for him.

"*Sanshō*? No, no, we don't have that. It's for eels."

"It's for rich-flavored meat as well. *Grillade* or *brochette*."

"It's for eels. Spicy."

His insistence that *sanshō* was strictly for eels struck me as ironic since a stack of eels occupied the entire lower left shelf of his freezer. So why no *sanshō*? I was too naïve to look for Sichuan pepper, and I wasn't going to argue about a common ingredient or bring up boars. Before giving up and heading over to Chinatown in the Thirteenth Arrondissement, I managed to find a package of *konbu* because "Natural Kelp" was printed among the characters. I went to the refrigerated shelves, which abounded with unfamiliar products, and found the *konnyaku*, made from an Asian yam processed in two forms, a pasta and a gelled block. I wanted to try them both. The miso paste came in a packet big enough to supply a restaurant for several months. The mushrooms weren't labeled, but I could easily recognize them.

Feeling pleased about my acquisitions, I showed each to Mary upon my return. She turned the block of *konnyaku* over and back again and asked, "So how do you plan to make this? There isn't even a word of French on here."

"I guess I'll cut it in strips."

She began turning over another package. "But you can't read the directions on any of these."

"We'll taste and experiment as we go. How complicated could it be?"

"Maybe you can scan these packages and get someone to interpret them."

Our professor friend from Japan could help, but I wasn't about to put *konnyaku, konbu,* and miso paste in the scanner. Besides, while the Japanese are ceremonious in the preparation of their cuisine, I figured our version of *botan nabe* would be delicious even if we were in a sense reinventing it in France. Cooking leeks, cabbage, carrots, mushrooms, tofu, noodles, and wild boar in broth at the table with dipping sauces sounded simple enough and certainly fun for the fête in the country house. The broth would become imbued with the flavors of the vegetables, mushrooms, and boar as they are steeped in it. While bland in itself, the *konnyaku* was purported to absorb the delicate essence of the broth at the end of the meal. But one could use an assortment of noodles in the same way.

Since we didn't have an authentic *raku nabe* and a hearth, we would improvise with enamel Le Creuset pots and cheap electric hot plates. While often a miso broth is used, we opted for a kelp broth that reminded me of tea, but just a taste conjured the sea and the long strips of kelp dried by the harvesters.

The challenge remained of acquiring more boar meat and delivering it fresh to our cooks. It turned out that Leonilda and her husband had befriended Monsieur Menard, the manager of a *domaine de chasse* operated by a nearby aristocratic family. A former gendarmerie captain, Menard looked after the elegant accommodations and high-priced boar hunts for individuals and groups. I went to meet him for apéritifs with the Wainwrights the evening he delivered an entire boar thigh.

If ever a manager fit the part of a hunting director with an aristocratic flair, it was Menard. He appeared with an amber single-malt scotch in hand, dressed in impeccable country gentleman's apparel: fine leather, khaki-colored riding breeches, canary vest, and cubbing jacket. He seemed covered with pockets, and in each one he kept a different knife. He heard that a writer would be visiting, and on my arrival greeted me enthusiastically, asking me to recite a poem. With my feeble memory, I could only produce Basho's famous boar haiku:

> Even a wild boar
> With all other things
> Blew in this storm.

Menard began theatrically reciting a Villon poem that he loved. He took a sip of Scotch and launched into another by Valéry and could clearly have kept them coming all night. If he wrote poems himself, he might well have been a modern-day troubadour, given that he lived in a chateau and possessed a true talent for recitation, hardly what I was expecting from a former gendarme, even a captain.

The boar thigh would have certainly provided a sufficient quantity of meat along with the rib roast for our fête, but we didn't have a loin, the cut of choice for *botan nabe*. Mary and I ventured to our village *boucherie* to see if we could order boar. Monsieur Saget assured us that he could have a loin from Rungis by week's end. He also offered to make several cuts from the boar thigh, which was still covered in fur. We were becoming spoiled.

True to his word, Monsieur Saget had transformed the thigh into a roast and stew meat that Leonilda planned to use. He also cut up the bone for a *fond*. That Friday afternoon, Mary and I made the rounds to our friends and delivered beautifully prepared boar cuts.

Our fête du sanglier was set for Sunday. I imagined the affair as mixing the rustic pleasures of a rural game feast with the *dîner de chasse* and the etiquette and gaiety of a banquet. After all, it wasn't so long ago that the social strata of France included these polarities. What we got, however, was a kitchen transformed by ever-increasing levels of pandemonium.

Jean-Michel's dish was so ambitious that he came over to start cooking at midday, occupying the stove's four burners while pots and dishes piled up in the sink. Fortunately *botan nabe* was simple to make, just a matter of careful chopping and presentation. When the Harveys arrived in the evening, a heavy stew pot in hand, and Leonilda showed up with her contribution, we had four cooks in a cramped space with one stove and virtually no counter area to spare.

To make matters worse, we hardly had space to seat ten in our dining room, and I had invited twelve. Chaos would have progressed into full-blown apocalypse except that Leonilda and the Harveys' dishes were, for the most part, prepared in advance. Our friends squeezed in and worked circles around each other. We lacked the luxuries of the "Kitchen Stadium" with just two iron chefs, each with two assistants. But we could certainly sympathize with their having to cook ten different dishes in one hour.

We quickly came to the conclusion that boar dishes should be served one at a time with a brief repose between, giving the chefs time and elbow room for final preparations in the kitchen. In addition, guests could pace themselves. Our upstairs loft was transformed into a makeshift concert hall, and apéritifs were set up in the salon while my mother put out hors d'oeuvres.

In late autumn, the days are abbreviated, the light contracted, the body seems to seek metaphorical light sources: music, wine, caloric food, and friends in high spirits. Mary and Leonilda worked through a musical menu of Marcello, Fauré, Caix d'Herlevois, and Diabelli for piano and cello. The concert was a pleasurable throwback to a time when homes had pianos, and friends played music for each other. The short performance ended with a demand for an encore.

Vitteau-Alberti was poured, igniting lively conversation. Had we been hunters at a rural game feast or the banquet, we would bask in recent hunting glories, relating the minutiae of the kill. Instead, we discussed the novelty of cooking boar.

For the first dish, we transcended reveries of European tradition when we brought the spirit of Kyoto to deep rural France. Mary and I started two hot pots for the *botan nabe,* one on a hot plate and the other a modified fondue stand. A maximum of four people could cook comfortably at one pot, and we had six at each. Communal cooking would look more like dueling chopsticks and fencing forks and spoons among the maladroit.

Mary had cut up two peonies' worth of boar loin to go with a decorative plate of mushrooms, leeks, cabbage, carrots, tofu, and noodles. We experimented with three different dipping sauces. The first was a traditional red miso paste dissolved in broth with just a sprinkling of *sanshō*. Then we tried a *ponzu* that included soy, lemon juice, rice wine vinegar, and *dashi* stock. *Dashi* comes from dried tuna and fish essence but imparted a light, smoky flavor. Finally, we made a typical Chinese dipping sauce version of soy with grated fresh garlic and ginger.

The water with sheets of *konbu* made a tealike broth when it came to a simmer. I added some soy sauce and sake, fearing the broth would have a fishy taste, but this wasn't the case at all. The *konbu* provided a delicate background as the broth assumed the flavors of mushrooms, leeks, cabbage, and boar meat. The thin slices of boar were surprisingly tender and were more flavorful than pork or beef, which are also used in *nabes*. We tested small helpings of tofu, *konnyaku*, and soba noodles to soak up the broth. The subtle, almost bland flavors were enlivened by the dipping sauces. In the end, we poured some of the sauces over the noodles. We served a red Chassagne Montrachet instead of the more customary sake or beer.

The Harveys had found a late medieval French boar recipe: *bourbelier de sanglier*, a loin of wild boar in boar's tail sauce. The combination of spices was based on the opening of trade routes to the East, first with the Arabs, later with the Portuguese, then with the Dutch and English. These spices include ginger, cinnamon, cardamom, pepper, cloves, and nutmeg. One could quickly surmise that this version of *bourbelier de sanglier* was not exactly peasant food. The medieval texts didn't provide weights and measures, so the modern-day version would be a refinement with unincorporated ingredients from the Americas, such as cayenne.

In this *bourbelier*, the boar loin is marinated for a day in red wine, lemon, and wine vinegar and then roasted on the spit or in a casserole, the marinade reduced and added at the end. The Harveys also used crème fraîche and currant jelly. The *bourbelier* was a profound shift from the nuanced vegetable and mushroom flavors of the *botan nabe:* it was a robust meat dish with cream, spices, and berries. We opened a Santenay red.

Our friend Corine was already dizzy on wine by the time Leonilda served a classic *cinghiale ragù* on fettuccini, which was an enormous hit. Leonilda grew up in a large second-generation Italian America family, and cooking always occupied a central place in her life. She had recently traveled to Umbria to attend the culinary school Villa di Monte Solare. When our fête was proposed, she researched two recipes — one from the rock star Brian Ritchie appearing in a book by Kara Zuaro, and the other by Emeril Lagasse — and improvised a combination of the two based on intuition and the ingredients we had available.

As one might expect with essentially a Bolognese sauce, the boar is browned in olive oil with sautéed onions. Then tomatoes, garlic, herbs, chili, wine, and wine vinegar are added. The recipe is lent a complexity of flavors by the combination of bay leaf, clove, sage, oregano, and basil. Richie's *ragù* also includes anchovies. The key is simmering the boar meat until it is tender: at least two hours until the meat absorbs the fluid and easily flakes apart. Leonilda's *ragù* was served over fettuccini, cooked al dente, accompanied by grated pecorino, the sheep cheese that is preferred with game. Our guests spontaneously applauded Leonilda's dish, perhaps extra-enthusiastically because of the hearty Côte de Beaune we drank.

Mary and I had watched Jean-Michel as he cooked all afternoon with us. My mother, a former scientist, says that biologists often make wonderful cooks, combining a keen sense of chemistry with imaginative experimentation. Jean-Michel used the boar rib roast that Jean-Marie Boisgibault had given us to make *sanglier au chocolat* and three purées: chestnut, celery root, and apple. Jean-Michel, however, used the bones to prepare a *fond,* which he reduced and then added blood and some chocolate. He browned the meat and then added the *mirepoix* that he had prepared: carrots, shallots, and leeks cooked long enough in butter with low heat that they caramelized. He added the sauce and reduced it further over low heat while he prepared the three purées.

All of us considered Jean-Michel's contribution worthy of a starred restaurant. It was by far the most refined and subtle of our four dishes, and it proved sanglier was indeed suitable for French haute cuisine. He brought an Aloxe Corton, an elegant Burgundy with an aroma of forest berries, to pair with his preparation. Our group broke out into a final round of applause.

Jean-Marie Boisgibault would have been astonished by how his boar rib roast had been transformed into such a superb dish. Likewise, he'd have been amused by how his neighborly gift triggered the idea for an adventurous culinary evening. Perhaps the fête didn't measure up to a Nero-era gluttonous banquet as described by Petronius: nevertheless, our evening was lit up with lively spirits on a late November night. One can easily imagine how the boar became associated with light in Norse mythology, the sacred animal of Frey, the god of Yule, renewal, the return of the sun from darkness. It would all begin with the wild pig of prosperity. While we paid homage to the remarkable animal, the black beast that rules our forests, we all agreed to eat and drink to shameless excess.

Chapter Fourteen

Julie

I HAVE SOMETHING that I know you will like," Evelyne said. "I'll bring it to you next weekend."

"What is it?" I asked, assuming it might be a book or photograph. "You'll see."

Jean-Marie offered no clues, only one of his cagey half-smiles. We were seated on a freshly built porch, part of a large addition Jean-Marie's team had constructed. Our friends, celebrating Jean-Marie's good works, prepared a generous buffet of cheeses and charcuterie and plied us with *crémant*.

I had forgotten about Evelyne's mysterious offer until, on the following Saturday morning, she startled me at our garden gate. Seeming in a rush, she presented me with a videocassette and said, "I'll tell you the story of Julie later." She urged me to give her warm regards to Mary and my mother and left. "Julie August 1999" was written in attractive script on the adhesive label.

I hooked up our neglected VCR, and a soundless home film flicked on, tremulous camera work swept to the Boisgibaults and a group of friends on an ordinary midday summer stroll, just a trek through a nearby woods. The group consisted of a boy in a red T-shirt and generic baseball cap, a more studiously dressed blond girl of about ten, an older couple, and finally Evelyn and Jean-Marie, younger by a decade. Jean-Marie — with his red, collarless shirt unbuttoned to his stomach Italian style — and the boy walked ahead of the others. Evidently the boy's mother was behind the video camera. One element that was anything but ordinary: Jean-Marie strolled ahead, a stick in hand, followed by his loyal dog that was not a dog at all but instead a stout young wild boar. This was Julie, wagging her tail busily, trotting along, in constant motion that could only be interpreted as animal joy — a wild boar on a family outing!

When Julie wasn't plowing her snout through some sod, she was trying to stick it in the lens of the video camera, either fond of the camerawoman or curious as to whether the camera was edible. One friend patted Julie's flanks between his hands, and even the blond girl ventured a cautious pat on Julie's shoulder. Julie galloped to catch up with Jean-Marie, who scratched her back with his stick, a sensation that seemed to mesmerize her with pleasure.

When the group rested, Jean-Marie and the boy sat on a pile of limestone rubble at the edge of a meadow, and Julie circled them, nosing about their feet, before flopping on her side like an enormous cat while Jean-Marie rubbed her behind the ears and on the stomach. The next scene showed the boy running and hiding behind an oak tree in a copse, and after Julie's probing snout once again eclipsed the camera lens she dashed off directly to the boy, as if she could see straight through the solid trunk of an oak. When the entourage arrived at a *mare* (often referred to in French as a *mare aux canards*), a swampy duck pond, she waded into the greenish opaque water to wallow while Jean-Marie and the boy waded along the near shore in rubber boots. Julie glided into deeper water, almost amphibious.

The last scene showed Julie's enclosure in the woods, the ground uniformly rooted up and muddy. Her corrugated steel shelter was sturdy enough for a woodsman to live in. Jean-Marie, a passionate fisherman, would put his catch into a rubber mortar tub transformed into Julie's feeding trough. The fish were so lively that Julie struggled to catch them, finally placing a hoofed toe on tails and biting the heads first to subdue them. Having emptied her tub of fish, she grazed on her more passive pile of cracked corn. In a ten-minute shaky home video, Julie had exhibited a startling array of wild-boar habits, all in the society of the Boisgibaults and their friends rather than within the matriarchal structure of a sounder.

Christmas was coming around again. Mary and I had put aside some money to install double-glazed windows to make our old house more energy-efficient and environmentally sound. We stopped by Boisgibaults' office to see if the work could be done before the holidays, a doubtful proposition since the windows had to be custom-built to match the irregularities of an eighteenth-century stone building. Evelyne had been busy with some paperwork, and the office lights were off, so that at first we couldn't tell whether she was there or not. We caught each other's shadowy attention, and she waved us in.

"You were right, Evelyne," I said. "I adored the film. Who goes on a family promenade with a delightful sanglier like Julie?" I'd seen sepia postcards with the family cat riding the back of a wild boar, women in the middle of villages hand-feeding them, and family dachshunds playing with a striped piglet. A 1955 photo-essay of a Frenchman with his wild boar, Arthur, had appeared in *Life* magazine. We see Arthur grabbing a cookie out of his owner's mouth and then getting a kiss on the snout and a hug as if he were *Porcellino* come to life. We see him marching dutifully down a village street to go fishing with his owner and his spaniel, onlookers marveling at the trio.

Performing boars will jump through hoops, play soccer, walk tightrope (more like a balance bar), race, and climb ladders. Except for the jittery amateur camera work and the snout continually blacking out the lens, Julie could have been a star in a children's story, but Evelyne had a different tale to tell.

The Boisgibaults' son found Julie as an orphaned marcassin after a hunt. While hunters are forbidden to shoot the *laie meneuse,* the ringleader sow, or *laie suitée,* a sow followed by piglets, it does happen. Heavy fines are accorded, and hunting privileges revoked for a year. The little ones can't survive without the compagnie, particularly in the cold weather of the hunting season. Jean-Marie constructed Julie's enclosure in the woods, but it is not legal to keep wild animals without authorization and regulation.

Evelyne explained, "Julie just grew too big for us to handle, so Jean-Marie brought her to the Parc Naturel Saint-Hubert de Boutissaint, where they keep boars for public viewing. Unfortunately, she didn't fit

A man walking his pet dog and pet boar, Arthur, from *Life* magazine.
(© Frank Scherschel/Getty Images)

in well. She fought with the others, and she became pregnant but ended up killing all her young. That's the last we heard of her. We couldn't go back, you understand."

In the wild, boars rarely kill their young. Laies make assiduous, doting mothers that can be ferociously protective if they perceive a threat. Julie had no maternal training in boar hierarchy and social etiquette, and thus it's no wonder she struggled with the governing nuances of dominance and submission, the order that makes a sounder a vigorous unit built for survival.

Neighbors all knew now that I had developed a particular fondness for the wild boars in our region and that I had been out on both rainy and freezing moonlit nights with them. Folks were eager to share their boar stories, some sending me newspaper clippings on boar invasions of city suburbs, airports, and cemeteries. Others were suspicious, concerned that they'd end up the object of antihunting ridicule. Evelyne knew that Julie would charm me.

Yet the Julie story was disturbing, an easy cautionary tale of human contact with a wild animal throwing her out of psychological and meta-physical balance. Julie fit in with neither human nor boar society, and as a result became deranged enough to kill her own young. Wildlife managers repeat the same warning: human communion with wild animals cripples them. Deer become addicted to candy; boars to hamburgers and French fries. We precipitate their fall in the *scala naturae*, the Great Chain of Being.

Monsieur Delanoe would shake his head and smile cynically over the domestic versus wild debate. He argues that we didn't have a boar problem in our region until the overplanting of corn crops and the development of large-scale mechanized farming. Our corn feeds the boars at the edge of managed forests, and they are culled before the age of three. When considered in this light, how different are wild boars from livestock? Some would argue that they are in fact lucky; free-range farm animals. Though their end is violent and terror-filled, particularly when pursued by dogs, their killing provides pleasure and passion to a certain few, even creating a sense of a rural season, the sport of hunting full of tradition, ceremony, even nostalgia. Unfortunate farm beasts simply queue up for the stun gun.

Julie's being brought to the Parc Naturel Saint-Hubert de Boutis-saint gave me a sinking feeling. This park is a nature conservatory established on the grounds of a thirteenth-century priory consecrated to Notre-Dame de Boutissaint. Families can enjoy watching waterbirds or fishing on three spring-fed lakes or walking the oak-forest trails, where the startling appearance of a deer herd, or perhaps a troupe of sangliers, offers a thrill. As at Chambord, the animals are kept in semi-liberty, meaning they are provided with supplemental feeding to support the large population density. Meanwhile, European bison, mouflon, and numerous types of deer are kept in smaller enclosures while goats, peacocks, and geese patrol the parking lot. Even small albino deer will venture out of the woods to graze on the priory's lawn, or at least the sections spared by moles and their astounding dirt eruptions. The geese pose the most aggressive threat, lowering their heads and charging with full-throttled honking, sending parents and children alike into adrenalin-driven retreat. By comparison, the Burgundian boar, the animal of violent myths, seems mostly docile. Still the boar *enclos* is, by far, the most impressive of the animal displays.

A few years back, Alexander, from Mary's extended family, stayed with us, and for a diversion we walked the grounds at the Parc Naturel Saint-Hubert de Boutissaint and watched the animals. A well-shaded area with tall perimeter fencing, the *enclos des sangliers* contained boars of all sizes and ages. The ground was barren, muddy and well-trodden, the bark on the trees worn by persistent scratching. Because mature adults had dug out so many pits for their diurnal siestas, the ground resembled a cratered battlefield. In clusters of boar bomb holes, we saw large furry ears sticking up, black backs hunched, and long snouts with jutting tusks resting on the rim. The young *rousses*, their red fur still showing the vestiges of their stripes, were far less sedentary, nosing the earth in groups, playing rough-and-tumble games that one day will lead to sorting out social rank and dominance.

They came running up to us, curious, entirely inured to the presence of humans and our camera. The tan-striped *marcassins* stumbled over each other trying to keep up with their mothers. One mature female approached Alexander and me for some patting or scratching, but we refrained, ignorant of boars at the time and wary of a possible bite.

We also caught the attention of one scraggly, vigilant older male boar with a single, very large tusk that curled back so fully it nearly circled itself. Twice it made an unexpected charge at us, causing us to recoil from the fence. The young female, though, paid no attention to all the posturing and false drama. She spent a half hour with us, and in that time we developed an affection for her. She raised her snout, looking us in the eyes, her short, stubby tusks pushing up the corners of her mouth, giving her an appealing boar smile.

Alexander visited again a few months later, this time with his cousin. After walking the shoreline of Lac Bourdon on an unusually sunny winter day, we checked the Parc Naturel Saint-Hubert de Boutissaint to see if it was open for the holiday season. Remarkably, it was. But as we drove up, we saw a bus chartered for transporting hunters. A pile of large deer, each with its legs roped together in the air, had been deposited on the lawn in front of the priory. It was as though hostages had been shot. I reversed the moment I saw the carnage, but it was too late; the children saw it and fell momentarily silent.

During the autumn/winter seasons, the nature park is transformed into one of the largest hunting reserves in France, with 3,500 acres divided into three parks. On designated Sundays, after breakfast, hunters participate in three battues, one in each park. After a long day of camaraderie and shooting, they gather with apéritifs in hand and, by torchlight, enjoy a view of the *tableau de chasse,* the game animals arranged on the lawn for a formal display. Each can point out his or her quarry, swap embellished stories about the moment of the kill. A hunting-horn concert adds an extra touch of tradition.

After Television France 2's *30 millions d'amis* ran a segment called "A Sunday in the Country" lauding the Parc Naturel Saint-Hubert de Boutissaint as an ideal family attraction for young children to enjoy the richness of nature, the station received a great outpouring of furious messages, forcing the management to write a mea culpa. The programmers hadn't properly researched the hunting operation: "Each program we show is the object of painstaking enquiry. However, it happens sometimes that despite this rigor we can be abused." It was an apology of sorts, but in reality the management merely transferred the blame to the park.

I would visit the park a number times but never with quite the previous naïve pleasure. I invariably returned to the *enclos des sangliers* to look for the boar that probably wasn't Julie. It may have been just another family-raised boar. Also I had hoped to see the boar with a single tusk, even though I'm sure the sentiment wasn't mutual. Each year the population of boars changed, with many fewer boars on my last visit. I recognized none of them. The boars that I'd seen no doubt garnered much-needed revenue since the Parc Naturel Saint-Hubert de Boutissaint is a private operation. The owners' entrepreneurial spirit led them even into the bed-and-breakfast business and beagle breeding.

Our new year began with abnormally frigid weather. Outdoor animals literally had frost in their fur, reminiscent of the salt boar. I had collected many pictures of boars in the snow, and one hung over my desk. We received snow cover that lingered over a week, temperatures never rising above freezing. Snow rarely lasts in our area. As I was jogging one morning, I noticed that the snow had recorded the crisscrossing tracks of dense animal traffic. It occurred to me that the snow would reveal areas of the most recent and extensive boar activity.

I spent an afternoon locating boar runs, perfect prints, the two main toes with the vestigial toes splayed behind. The runs and the rooting were just where I expected to find them along the rue des Postillons. I found extensive boar activity around several of the reservoirs, but nowhere as densely as at the Étang du Château, where I had spent so many nights listening and waiting for boars.

The evening was mystical. I stood on the frozen shore of the Étang du Château, listening to the darkening woods, to the stillness, which, to be honest, was not so still. I heard heavy treading, not of boars but blackbirds called *merles*. While *merles* provide some of the purest notes in the spring, here they made quite a racket thrashing through the leaves. As I'd approach, they'd burst into flight, sounding alarms through the woods even as the sun burned out among the bare black trees on the far side of the frozen lake.

The chateau turned mauve with a hint of orangish pink on the turrets before assuming a uniform gray. The snow had made a pristine canvas on the lake — pristine, that is, except for a striking variety of animal tracks: rabbits, mice, nutria, ducks, and dogs. I passed the peninsula and saw the lift-off pattern of a great blue heron recorded on the lake. It was as if someone had whipped palm fronds on the snow, and it made me think how difficult life must be for herons in a deep freeze.

Boars had torn up the shoreline, making massive gouges through the snow and leaves into the frozen earth, a tribute to the exceptional power of their snouts. They didn't venture far onto the lake. Though they can swim, burrow, and practically fly through thickets, they can't negotiate ice. Where they hit ice, they leave splayed skid marks from hooves that give them no traction whatsoever.

Wild Boar in the Moonlight (ca. 1818–30), scroll painting by Katsushika Hokusai.
(Photograph © 2011, Museum of Fine Arts, Boston)

A perfect full moon rose over the frosty woodlands. I could feel the temperature dropping to −8°C, as I later learned. I walked to the edge of a crater in the woods away from the lake. One of the classic boar images in Japanese art shows a boar traversing snow under a full moon. Hokusai was fond of rendering boars in prints and paintings. In the figure of the isolated boar, a kind of monastic loneliness is intensified by the spare, illuminated winter landscape, the boar looking up at the perfect disk suspended in space.

I had been so absorbed in the calm night settling that I was not prepared for a sudden loud squeal, heavy thrashing in the understory, and hooves charging across the ground. I had blundered rudely into a boar's lair. In a moment, a veering beast and a startled man met at the threshold of darkness and inner shock. Suddenly nothing was neutral, not the black trees, frigid lake, or sentient moon. We had almost touched.

Recipes

WILD BOAR

Although none of us had cooked boar before our first Christmas feast, afterward my mother wanted to try her hand at a sanglier dish. Counter to the ardent and repeated advice to marinate or stew the meat, however, she was determined to target its essential flavor. She had an idea that you could take a classic standing rib-roast recipe and make it even more sumptuous with young boar meat. She was right.

In the 1980s, the "low-fat diet" was triggered by fears that well-marbled, super-tender meat was responsible for obesity and heart disease. Public demand grew for white, lower-cholesterol, lower-calorie meats such as skinless chicken breasts and lean pork. In response, the pork industry, particularly in the United States, has mass-produced nearly flavorless pork. Tastes change, though; nowadays, there is a demand for organic, richer-tasting meats. Even the Japanese are conducting meat-science studies on wild boar/domestic pig mixes aimed at achieving attractive, rich, red coloration and quality muscle fiber to go with the versatility and high production yield of pork.

Championing the essential flavor of organic food is becoming increasingly common among food writers like Michael Pollan and superb chefs like Daniel Barber, who created Blue Hill Restaurant in Manhattan. Barber runs his own organic farm in New York State to supply produce for his restaurants, virtually erasing the distance between where food is produced and the plate. In raising animals, Barber's goal is to create free-range conditions for the flavor of the meat, the health of the animal, and the protection of the environment. "We try to mimic the conditions of the wild boar or wild animal," he says. "That's the name of the game."

My mother, who cooked with Barber when he first started realizing his culinary gifts, completely agreed with his methods. Wild boar is flavorful organic food from our backyard. With good-quality pork, my mother's simple dish is exceptional, the key being to get an herb and butter mixture between the bone and the loin.

Roast Loin of Boar/Pork with Herbs
Serves 5 to 6

3- to 4-pound loin, bone-in
¼ pound butter
¼ cup each chopped fresh sage and parsley
2 tablespoons each chopped fresh thyme and rosemary
2 to 3 tablespoons minced garlic
Salt and freshly ground pepper

1. Keeping your knife close to the bone, cut a channel through the loin.
2. Mix chopped herbs and minced garlic with the butter (olive oil will do nicely too). Push the mixture in the hole you've made until it's full.
3. If there is a layer of fat (desired for crispy, succulent skin) on the outside of the roast, make tiny parallel cuts through the fat over the whole roast and rub the butter/herb mixture into the surface of the roast, making sure to get it into all the little cuts. Then salt and pepper.
4. Roast at medium to high heat for 20 to 25 minutes to the pound or until 150° to 160°F at the thickest part of the meat.

JABALÍ

Jeff Koehler is a compulsive world traveler who earns his living as a journalist, photographer, and cookbook writer. Though he is based in Barcelona, we met in Paris and quickly developed a correspondence when I asked about wild boars in Spain. He assured me that Spanish boars were plentiful and mischievous, frequently startling cyclists in northern sections of Barcelona and wreaking havoc in the olive groves. They were not eating olives, but rather chewing through irrigation lines for a cool drink and a soothing wallow. Cities in Spain were experiencing boar invasions similar to those in France and Germany. Even David Beckham, the soccer great, and his wife, former Spice Girl Victoria, had boars in their yard in a luxury neighborhood in Madrid.

Jeff's messages were filled with sumptuous descriptions of meats, fish, grains, and herbs. He'd recount his recipe experiments inspired by textures, colors, seasonings, and ingredients in cuisine he experienced on his travels. A dish sometimes evolves out of invention and inspired memory. In one message, he described his method: "I am not an expert but an interested observer. Call me a jackdaw, a culinary jackdaw who picks up scraps here and there on my travels. Jackdaws also, from my understanding, are one of the few animals that share food and building material: so perhaps the metaphor is particularly fitting."

Could I resist asking Jeff to invent a boar recipe in keeping with a sense of Spanish tradition?

He was glad to work on it, though fitfully at first because of his heavy workload. His recipe, he announced, would be an adobo, a traditional *jabalí* stew, but in this case for a *tapa*. He wrote, "We love and eat it often (in various ways), or else a similar way of preparing called *escabeche/ escabetx*"—a spiced garlicky marinade.

"It is a matter of finding the right spices but also working with a new meat which reacts differently—wild boar is not farm-raised pork. One of the recipes I looked at is from a bar in Andalucía. The owner gave it to me a few years ago when I was working on a tapas piece for *Food and Wine*. And, of course, I found another dozen or more, all variations with *jabalí*. It is a matter of tinkering until I find what in my mouth's imagination I'd hoped to achieve."

Jeff's "mouth's imagination" often works from memory, but in this case, he mixed in tradition. "I'm working forward, not backward, if that makes sense."

Jabalí en adobo/Boar in Spanish *adobo*
Serves 6 to 8 as part of a selection of tapas

4 cloves garlic, peeled
3 teaspoons Spanish *pimentón* (sweet paprika)
2 teaspoons ground cumin
1 teaspoon dried oregano
½ cup white wine
¼ cup wine vinegar
6 tablespoons extra-virgin olive oil
1 pound slightly fatty stewing boar meat,
    cut into 1-inch-square pieces
Salt and freshly ground pepper
1 bay leaf
1 cup water

1. In a food processor, blend the garlic, *pimentón,* cumin, oregano, wine, vinegar, and 4 tablespoons of the oil.
2. Place the boar in a glass bowl and mix with this marinade. Cover, refrigerate, and let marinate overnight.
3. Drain the boar, reserving the marinade. Pat the meat dry with paper towels.
4. In a terra-cotta or cast-iron *cazuela* (casserole) or heavy skillet, heat the remaining 2 tablespoons of the oil over medium heat. Season the boar with salt and pepper and add. Cook, turning occasionally, until browned, about 5 minutes.
5. Pour in the reserved marinade and add the bay leaf. Bring to a boil, reduce heat to low, and simmer until the wine in the marinade has reduced, about 20 minutes. Add the water and continue to simmer until the meat is tender, 20 to 30 minutes.
6. Remove the bay leaf and discard. Transfer the boar to a plate, spoon over the sauce, and serve.

This is a tapa so the *jabalí abodo* would be accompanied by other dishes. Jeff wrote, "Perhaps *pimientos del piquillo.* Or *morcilla de Burgos* (that has rice and onions inside)? Fitting would be some *pintxos* made with bread rounds topped by a round of fried *morcilla* topped with a fried quail egg." Jeff also suggests a young red wine, fruity and with a hint of spice.

INOSHISHI

One of the oldest and most practical cooking methods in eastern Asia is the hot-pot stew. It is a form of communal hearth cooking that offers both heat and nourishment in the cold, mountainous regions of Mongolia, Korea, Vietnam, and Japan. Since the vegetables, meats, and fish are cooked quickly *nabemono*-style, and the broth is absorbed in noodles or provides a soup, there is little nutritional loss.

The communal hot pot resembles the participatory experience of eating cheese, beef, or chocolate fondue in our part of the world; but it provides a generally low-fat, healthy meal that includes a variety of mushrooms and vegetables. *Botan nabe* is the wild-boar version of the hot pot. It is an unusual dish, even in Japan, and is found mainly in the Kyoto area, where butchers who specialize in game can be found. *Botan nabe* is eaten in the autumn and winter, when wild boars put on the fat that helps them through the cold season and facilitates reproduction.

This is a pleasing dish to share with friends. Sliced pork shoulder, marbled beef, or duck breast can be substituted for wild boar, but the rich forest flavor will be missed.

Botan nabe
Serves 4

For the broth:
4 cups of water
1 cup *konbu* (dried kelp that comes in sheets or strips)
2 tablespoons soy sauce
1 cup sake

Meat and vegetables:
1 pound wild boar, very thinly sliced against the grain
2 cups Chinese cabbage cut first in quarters and then in
    ½-inch slices
2 young leeks sliced cut in 2-inch pieces then sliced
    lengthwise in four strips
3 carrots, julienned
4 to 6 shiitake mushrooms
4 generous clusters of enoki mushrooms
4 long scallions, cut in 2-inch pieces
1 cake of firm or medium firm tofu cut into bite-size strips
2 packages of *udon* noodles
½ cup *konnyaku* cut in strips (*konnyaku* also comes in the
    form of *shirataki* noodles)

For the dipping sauce — ponzu *(for each serving):*
5 tablespoons soy sauce
5 tablespoons *dashi* (a bonito stock)
1 tablespoon lemon juice
2 tablespoons rice vinegar

1. The aesthetic presentation of *botan nabe* is as important as its
   savors. Cut the boar meat in thin petal-like slices and arrange on
   a plate in the form of a flower.
2. Prepare either a central platter or individual plates with the vegetables, tofu, mushrooms, and noodles divided into colorful groups.
3. Ideally, *botan nabe* broth is cooked in a special *raku* pot over a flame,
   but any medium-sized pot will do. Bring water, *konbu* seaweed,
   sake, and soy sauce to a simmer. Preparing the broth is a bit like
   making tea. Once the *konbu* has steeped, remove it.
4. For the *ponzu* dipping sauce, simply mix in a small bowl the soy
   sauce, *dashi*, lemon juice, and rice wine vinegar.
5. Start by adding the cabbage, carrots, leeks, scallions, and mushrooms to the stock, followed by *konnyaku* and tofu. Take out veg-

etables with chopsticks and dip them in the sauces as you eat. Place the slices of boar meat in the hot pot to cook (be aware that you may wish to dip them in the broth, as they will cook quickly). The trick is to avoid overcooking the ingredients. Finally, add the *udon* noodles to absorb the broth.

WILDSCHWEIN

Texas Parks and Wildlife (TPW) has entered the business of posting recipes, including one for wild-boar schnitzel. One might jump to the conclusion that TPW would like to entice the public into mass consumption of their number-one animal outlaw, the feral hog. But, in fact, TPW provides a fairly sophisticated assortment of wild-game recipes, the wild-boar schnitzel among them, recalling the German-settler heritage especially in the Texas Hill Country. In German, the dish is called *Wildschweinschnitzel,* wild boar cutlet.

The Texas recipe has a distinct rancher's twist, calling for a spiced, garlicky rub and 1½ hours in the smoker. The recipe also calls for an apple brandy sauce. I asked my mother if she could bring the schnitzel recipe back to the Old World and make it with something from our own backyard.

We have apple trees, but my mother proposed a *mirabelle* spicy sweet-and-sour sauce since we were swamped with *mirabelles,* small golden plums that taste like honey. In a good year, the plums are so abundant and weighty that the branches bow to the ground and often split. Just from one small tree, we have more plums than we could possibly consume, so we conserve them. My mother decided that *Wildschweinschnitzel* provided an ideal culinary excuse to have a peppery sweet-and-sour flavoring on crisp, robust flavored cutlets.

Wildschweinschnitzel
Serves 4

---

1 pound boar loin
1 egg
2 teaspoons water
½ cup flour
¼ teaspoon black pepper
½ teaspoon salt
¼ cup vegetable oil
2 tablespoons sweet butter
1 cup fine bread crumbs

For the plum sherry sauce:
40 pitted *mirabelles* (or any other kind of plum,
    fewer for larger plums)
½ cup sherry
½ cup veal stock
1 tablespoon balsamic vinegar
¼ teaspoon cayenne pepper
    (just a pinch for those sensitive to hot pepper)
1 teaspoon sugar
¼ teaspoon salt

1. Slice boar loin against the grain to make half-inch cutlets. Place each cutlet between pieces of cling film and pound it thin without breaking the meat.
2. Remove and dredge each flatted cutlet in seasoned flour. Prepare an egg wash by mixing the egg with 2 teaspoons of water in a dish. Coat the dredged cutlets with the egg wash, and then cover them with bread crumbs. Place the breaded cutlets uncovered in the refrigerator for a half hour.
3. Prepare the sauce by placing the *mirabelles,* sherry, veal stock, balsamic vinegar, cayenne pepper, sugar, and salt in saucepan on a medium heat to reduce for 15 minutes.

4. Add butter and oil in a frying pan on medium-high heat and sauté the cutlets until brown and crisp. Pour sauce on a heated serving dish and place cutlets on top.

CINGHIALE

In many ways, wild boar ragù on fettuccini is the consummate boar dish — or at least the one boar dish most likely to please both adults and children. It is also, as mentioned before, the first boar dish most non-Europeans are likely to taste when visiting Italy. It is familiar to most because it is a cousin of pasta with a Bolognese sauce, but the boar meat is richer than beef and retains its meaty texture.

The recipe comes from the rock star Brian Ritchie of the the Violent Femmes. As Ritchie explains: "Making a *ragù* is like playing jazz. You have to be creative, tasteful, and able to adapt to the circumstances. The beauty of *ragù* is that everybody is free to develop their own." Ritchie assures us that this *ragù* can be made with lamb, pork, veal, beef, or venison. Some prefer to use less cinnamon as it can mask flavor.

Wild Boar Ragù

(From the book *I Like Food, Food Tastes Good* by Kara Zuaro; Copyright © 2007 Kara Zuaro; Reprinted by permission of Hyperion; All rights reserved.)

4 to 6 servings

---

1 large Spanish onion (chopped)
2 tablespoons olive oil
2 pounds boneless wild boar meat (cut for stew)
1 can chopped tomatoes
3 bay leaves
1 cup red wine
5 cloves garlic, crushed
3 dried chili peppers (crushed)
1 cinnamon stick
5 cloves

3 sun-dried tomatoes
3 anchovies or 1 teaspoon anchovy paste
Fresh or dried oregano, basil, and sage
1 tablespoon red wine vinegar
Salt and black pepper to taste
Pasta (pappardelle or fettuccine)
Grated pecorino cheese (Parmigiano is an acceptable substitute,
   but pecorino, being sheep cheese, complements game.)

1. In a large cast-iron pot, sauté the onion in olive oil until translucent.
2. Add the boar meat and brown. (That is, cook the meat over high
   heat, turning frequently, just until it's cooked on the outside.)
3. Add the canned tomatoes and the bay leaves.
4. Add the wine.
5. Gradually add the garlic, dried chili, cinnamon stick, cloves, sun-
   dried tomatoes, anchovies (or anchovy paste), oregano, basil, sage,
   red wine vinegar, and salt and black pepper to taste.
6. Simmer on low on the stovetop with the lid of the pot slightly ajar,
   and stir occasionally for at least 2 hours — or longer if possible. The
   longer you simmer this, the more tender the meat will become. The
   ragù is ready to eat when the meat has totally fallen apart and most
   of the liquid has been absorbed by the meat. Take out the cinnamon stick and bay leaves before serving.
7. Serve over the pasta and top with grated cheese. Accompany with
   some crusty peasant bread and a good red wine, preferably a strong
   Italian, like Amarone or Barolo.

Mangia!

SANGLIER

My passion for wildlife and the natural world comes from growing up
in the New England woods. After the age of ten, I lived in a succession
of cities, but finally in later life I was able to reconnect with *la forêt* in
France with the primal sensations: the filtered light; the odors of rot-

ted logs, humus, and mushrooms; and the leaves in sudden bursts that sound like applause on blustery days.

Mary, my mother, and I pondered dishes that would capture something of France, wild boar, and the woods of Burgundy. My mother proposed duxelles rolled in boar cutlets, sautéed, flamed, and served with a Burgundy wine sauce. "It's a *paupiette,*" she explained. Boars and mushrooms provide an ideal synergy of flavors, and since boars adore mushrooms and both have the earthy savor of the forest, what could be more fitting? Duxelles are made from finely minced mushrooms, both cultivated and wild, sautéed in butter with shallots and seasoning, all of which intensifies the flavor. Duxelles were the invention of the great seventeenth-century chef François Pierre de La Varenne, who revolutionized French cooking. It didn't escape our attention that de La Varenne was born in Burgundy!

Paupiettes de Sanglier
Serves 4

---

1 pound boar loin cutlets
1 pound white mushrooms
10 morels
5 small shallots, minced
½ cup red Burgundy wine
¼ cup brandy
4 tablespoons butter
¼ cup chopped parsley
1 tablespoon corn starch
½ cup veal stock
Caul (for wrapping cutlets, if preferred)
Salt and pepper to taste

1. Soak and clean morels. Then mince the white mushrooms and morels.
2. Melt half the butter in a sauté pan. Add minced shallots and mush-

rooms. Add salt and pepper to taste and stir until all the moisture evaporates and the mushrooms brown.

3. Add wine and continue to cook until the liquid in the mushroom mixture evaporates and the mixture browns again.

4. Slice four boar cutlets and place them in cling wrap. Pound them until thin without breaking the meat. Remove them, spread the mushroom mix on top of the cutlets, and roll the meat, pinning them with toothpicks or wrapping them in caul.

5. Dust the rolled cutlets with cornstarch, and with the remaining butter sauté in the pan until golden brown. Pour on brandy and flame.

6. Place the cutlets on a plate. Deglaze the sauté pan with red wine, then add veal stock and cook until the sauce thickens. Season with salt and pepper to taste. Pour a small stream of sauce simply to moisten the cutlets, and serve the rest in a sauceboat.

SOURCES AND ACKNOWLEDGMENTS

This book records a personal journey into the world of the wild boar, one of our most intelligent, visually striking, and historically and culturally significant animals. With no expertise but driven by a deep curiosity, I consulted a range of articles and texts. The following is a list (in order of appearance) of poems, songs, tracts, letters, and film from which I have quoted: Snorri Sturluson, *The Prose Edda*, trans. Jessie L. Byock (London: Penguin Classics, 2005); Robinson Jeffers, "Steelhead, Wild Pig, The Fungus," in *The Selected Poetry of Robinson Jeffers*, ed. Tim Hunt (Palo Alto: Stanford University Press, 2001); "The bore's head in hande bring I," in *Ancient English Christmas Carols: 1400–1700*, by Edith Rickert (London: Chatto and Windus, 1910); Leon Battista Alberti, *On Painting* (New Haven: Yale University Press, 1966); Charles Darwin, *The Variation of Animals and Plants under Domestication*, 2nd ed., vol. 1 (London: John Murray, Albemarle Street, 1875); Bartholomaeus Anglicus, *De proprietatibus rerum*, bk. 18, ed. Robert Steele (London: Alexander Moring, 1893/1905); Robert Baden-Powell, *Lessons from the Varsity of Life* (London: C. Arthur Pearson, 1933); Pliny, *Natural History*, ed. John S. White (New York: G. P. Putnam's and Sons, 1885); Petronius, *Satyricon*, trans. Alfred R. Allinson (New York: Panurge Press, 1930); Ovid, *Metamorphoses*, trans. David Raeburn (London: Penguin, 2004); William Shakespeare, *Venus and Adonis*, in *The Riverside Shakespeare* (Boston: Houghton Mifflin, 1974); *The Pursuit after Diarmuid O'Duibhne, and Grainne, the Daughter of Cormac Mac Airt, King of Ireland in the Third Century*, ed. Standish Hayes O'Grady (Dublin: John O'Daly, 1857); Cervantes, *Don Quixote*, trans. J. M. Cohen (Baltimore: Penguin Books, 1964); *Home from the Hill* (Turner Entertainment Co. and Sol C. Siegel Productions, 1959); William Humphrey, *Home from the Hill* (Baton Rouge: LSU Press, 1996); George Gordon Moore to Stuyvesant Fish, "The Origin of Wild Boar in Monterey County," www.mchsmuseum.com/boar.html; Robinson Jeffers, "The Stars Go over the Lonely Ocean," in *The Selected Poetry of Robinson Jeffers*, ed. Tim Hunt (Palo Alto: Stanford University Press, 2001); Basho, *Selected Poems of Matsuo Basho*, trans. David Landis Barnhill (Albany: State University of New York Press, 2004).

Wild boars notoriously make their way into the newspaper headlines and magazine pieces. I have quoted from the following articles (in order of appearance): Ian Frazier, "Hogs Wild," *New Yorker*, 12 December 2005; C. J. Chivers,

"Tending to a Fallen Marine, with Skill, Prayer, and Fury," *New York Times,* 2 November 2006; Danielle Ring, "Hog-Dog Fights: Blood 'Sport' Packaged as Family Entertainment," Humane Society of the United States, 2 December 2004, www.humanesociety.org/issues/hogdogfighting/facts/hog-dog_blood sport.html; Joan Weibel-Orlando, "A Room of (His) Own: Italian and Italian-American Male-Bonding Spaces and Homosociality," *Journal of Men's Studies,* 22 March 2008; Miguel Bustillo, "It's a War on Boars, but Pork's Winning," *Los Angeles Times,* 19 November 2007; Shaila Dewan, "Tall Tales and the Unlarded Truth about Hogzilla," *New York Times,* 19 March 2005; Todd Spivak, "Hogs Wild," *Houston Press,* 24 August 2006; Kitty Crider, "The Boar War," *Austin Statesman,* 4 October 2006.

The following books have served as crucial resources: Milo Kearney, *The Role of Swine Symbolism in Medieval Culture: Blanc Sanglier* (Lewiston, Queenston, and Lampeter: Edwin Mellen Press, 1991); Étienne Pascal, *Le sanglier* (Paris: Delachaux et Niestlé, 2003); Jean Lavollée, *La chasse au sanglier en Puisaye* (La Ferte-sous-Jouarre: Geda Editions, 2005); Christian Trézan, *Château de Chambord* (Paris: Éditions du Patrimone, 2002); Laurent Cabanau, *Wild Boar in Europe,* trans. Nigel Suffield Jones (Cologne: Könemann, 2001); Pascal Durantel, *Chasser le sanglier* (Saint-Amand-Montrond: Editions Proxima); John J. Meyer and I. Lehr Brisbin Jr., *Wild Pigs in the United States* (Athens: University of Georgia Press, 2008); Michael Pollan, *The Omnivore's Dilemma* (London: Bloomsbury, 2006); Anne Gruet, *Le sanglier: Cuisine et saveurs* (Paris: Éditions de Montbel, 2005); Michael Pollan, *In Defense of Food* (New York: Penguin, 2008).

On this journey, I had numerous guides who made essential contributions. Among them, I particularly want to thank Dr. Martin Goulding, Roger Ramon, Laurent and Catherine Harvey, Jeff Koehler, Jean-Pierre Bajon, Jean-Marie and Evelyne Boisgibault, Françoise Vassallo, Francis Forget, and Corine Thuilier-Delahaie.

My deepest gratitude to Boyd Zenner, acquiring editor at the University of Virginia Press, whose enthusiasm for the subject, guidance, and tireless improvements to the text made this book possible. In addition, I am grateful to Angie Hogan, whose technical expertise was invaluable. I especially want to thank Laura Strahan, literary agent, who encouraged this offbeat project from its inception.

Special thanks to Susan Prospere, Bex Brian, Mary McFadden, John Baxter, Alexander Ephrussi, and Lee and Peter Wainwright for their support and inspiration.

Love and deepest thanks to my mother, Gretchen Van Blaricom, for contributing ideas and recipes and sharing numerous wild boar experiences.

INDEX